Sonar Code Quality Testing Essentials

Achieve higher levels of Software Quality with Sonar

Charalampos S. Arapidis

BIRMINGHAM - MUMBAI

Sonar Code Quality Testing Essentials

First published: August 2012

Production Reference: 1190812

Published by Packt Publishing Ltd.
Livery Place
35 Livery Street
Birmingham B3 2PB, UK.

ISBN 978-1-84951-786-7

www.packtpub.com

Cover Image by Asher Wishkerman (a.wishkerman@mpic.de)

Credits

Author
Charalampos S. Arapidis

Reviewers
Christopher Bartling
Efraim Kyriakidis
Kosmas Mackrogamvrakis
Lefteris Ntouanoglou

Acquisition Editor
Usha Iyer

Lead Technical Editor
Azharuddin Sheikh

Technical Editors
Prasad Dalvi
Veronica Fernandes
Manasi Poonthottam

Project Coordinator
Sai Gamare

Proofreader
Sandra Hopper

Indexer
Monica Ajmera Mehta

Graphics
Manu Joseph

Production Coordinators
Aparna Bhagat
Nilesh R. Mohite

Cover Work
Aparna Bhagat

About the Author

Charalampos S. Arapidis is a Senior Software Engineer located at Athens, Greece. He specializes in J2EE enterprise application design and implementation. His other specialties include data-mining/visualization techniques and tuning continuous integrated environments.

From a very early age, Charalampos showed particular interest in advanced Mathematics and software development and has been honored twice at the Panhellenic Mathematical Contest for providing prototype and innovative solutions. He graduated in Computer and Software Engineering from the Polytechnic School of the Aristotle University.

After graduation, he dynamically entered the enterprise field, where he helped his organization make the transition from legacy client server ERP and CRM applications to full-stack J2EE web applications, all in a streamlined and integrated development environment.

The development of the Proteus Web Document Management System for the Greek Public Sector and his solutions to Kallikratis — the largest data integration project ever conceived in the latter years of Greece's public sector — are two of his most recognizable achievements nationwide.

Charalampos currently works at Siemens Enterprise Communications as a Senior Software Applications Engineer, designing and implementing Unified Communications software at multinational level.

When not working he enjoys blogging, playing the classical guitar, and composing music, exploring new ways to translate polynomial equations to sound.

I would like to thank and express my gratitude to Lefteris Ntouanoglou for providing me with guidance and vision in the IT field especially in the last two years, and Olivier Gaudin and Fabrice Bellingard for their interest in the book. From the Packt Publishing staff, I would like to thank, in particular, Newton Sequeira, Ashwin Shetty, Sai Gamare, and Usha Iyer for supporting and guiding me through the writing process, and all the technical reviewers for their helpful suggestions. Finally, I would like to thank Kostas Vasiliou, Christos Chrysos, Vassilis Arapidis, and Evangelia Vlachantoni for their support.

About the Reviewers

Christopher Bartling has been in the IT industry since 1995. He has served in the roles of application developer, mentor, and agile coach. He also has experience in biometrics, genomics and computational biology, healthcare, insurance, and legal/regulatory domains. He also helps develop and deliver training for DevJam (http://www.devjam.com). Prior to his career in IT, he was involved in electrophysiology and biomedical research at the Mayo Clinic in Rochester Minnesota. You can find his blog at http://bartling.blogspot.com and tweets at @cbartling.

Efraim Kyriakidis is a skilled software engineer with over seven years of experience in developing and delivering software solutions for diverse customers. He's well versed in all stages of the software development lifecycle. His first acquaintance with computers and programming was a state-of-the-art Commodore 64, back in the '80s as a kid. Since then he has grown and received his Diploma in Electrotechnic Engineering from Aristotle University, Thessaloniki. Through his career, he mainly worked with Microsoft Technologies and has an interest in technologies such as Silverlight and Windows Phone. He currently works for Siemens AG in Germany as a Software Developer.

Kosmas Mackrogamvrakis was born in 1971 on the island of Crete in Greece. He moved at an early age to the capital of Greece, Athens. There he attended public school and graduated as an engineer in Automatic Electronics. Later, he continued his studies at the Technical School of Computers in Athens, but he was forced to interrupt, as he was obliged to join the army.

In the army he served as a Sergeant in the artillery section and trained in computer-guided canon targeting, based on his previous knowledge of computer technology.

Even before high school, he was highly interested in computer science, and he managed to learn Basic, Pascal, and Assembly language.

After his army obligations, he was employed by Athens News Agency, where he worked as a technician and desktop-publishing employee. There he was trained by Unibrain, in Ventura Publishing software, Photoshop, and Corel Draw. In parallel, he installed a Fax distribution network with Canada, for redistribution of a FAX newspaper.

After three years he moved to Hellenic Scientific S.A., as a technician. There he managed to get trained and show his natural talent in computer engineering. He was trained on the job and successfully undertook all the responsibilities of a Senior Systems Engineer after six years, and learned and used the following operating systems and software and services: Microsoft Windows 98/2000/XP/Vista, Microsoft Windows Server NT/2000/2003, Novel, Unix/Xenix, Mac OS/X, Linux, AIX, AS/400; Networks including WAN/LAN Protocols, TCP/IP, DNS, FTP, HTTP, IMAP/POP3, SMTP, VPN; E-mail systems Sendmail, Microsoft Exchange, Postfix, and clients such as Outlook, Mozilla Thunderbird, Kmail, and Evolution. He specialized in the hardware of IBM, HP, Dell, Fujitsu Servers, Desktops, and Notebooks.

He got certifications on Exchange Server from Microsoft, AIX from IBM, Tivoli IT Director from IBM, and AS/400 from IBM.

After seven years, and due to market needs and degradation of the company's share in the market, he moved to freelancing.

As a freelancer, he supported a large number of small-to medium-sized companies, as systems engineer, consultant, and technician.

Some of the companies that he was supporting included Rothmans, Adidas, Kraft Hellas, Vivechrom (Akzo), Public Sector (ministries and prefectures), Pan Systems.

After seven years of freelancing, he was asked by Siemens to undertake the position of Systems Engineer for the public sector and later Project Manager.

After three years in Siemens, the public sector IT support stopped in Greece, and he left the company.

Lately, and right after Siemens, he undertook the position of IT Services Manager for southeast Europe in Adidas.

Lefteris Ntouanoglou is a co-founder and the CEO of Schoox Inc, a Delaware company based in Austin, Texas, which developed schooX—a Social Academy for Self-learners (www.schoox.com). He has extensive administrative and management experience in the software sector. Prior to Schoox Inc, he joined a European startup company, OTS SA, which developed administrative and financial software for the Public Sector. He served the company from a various number of managerial positions and as the COO of the company he built one of the largest software companies in Greece.

During his PhD, he developed computer algorithms for fast computation of holographic patterns and graduated with Honor. In 1998, he was praised with the Award of Innovation from the Association of Holographic Techniques in Germany for inventing and implementing an innovative anticounterfeiting system based on a coded Holographic Label and a Web Application.

He is a highly skilled engineer and a visionary entrepreneur. Creativity and innovative thinking is part of his personality. Implementing new ideas and turning them into successful business by building and motivating strong and result-oriented teams is one of his strengths.

He was born and grew up in Germany and speaks fluent Greek, German, and English.

www.PacktPub.com

Support files, eBooks, discount offers and more

You might want to visit www.PacktPub.com for support files and downloads related to your book.

Did you know that Packt offers eBook versions of every book published, with PDF and ePub files available? You can upgrade to the eBook version at www.PacktPub.com and as a print book customer, you are entitled to a discount on the eBook copy. Get in touch with us at service@packtpub.com for more details.

At www.PacktPub.com, you can also read a collection of free technical articles, sign up for a range of free newsletters and receive exclusive discounts and offers on Packt books and eBooks.

http://PacktLib.PacktPub.com

Do you need instant solutions to your IT questions? PacktLib is Packt's online digital book library. Here, you can access, read and search across Packt's entire library of books.

Why Subscribe?

- Fully searchable across every book published by Packt
- Copy and paste, print and bookmark content
- On demand and accessible via web browser

Free Access for Packt account holders

If you have an account with Packt at www.PacktPub.com, you can use this to access PacktLib today and view nine entirely free books. Simply use your login credentials for immediate access.

To my parents, Simeon Arapidis and Ioanna Tsonona

Table of Contents

Preface

Developers continuously strive to achieve higher levels of source code quality. It is the holy grail in the software development industry. Sonar is an all-out platform confronting quality from numerous aspects as it covers quality on seven axes, provides an abundance of hunting tools to pinpoint code defects, and continuously generates quality reports following the continuous inspection paradigm in an integrated environment. It offers a complete and cost-effective quality management solution, an invaluable tool for every business.

Sonar is an open source platform used by development teams to manage source code quality. Sonar has been developed with this main objective in mind: make code quality management accessible to everyone with minimal effort. As such, Sonar provides code analyzers, reporting tools, manual reviews, defect-hunting modules, and Time Machine as core functionalities. It also comes with a plugin mechanism enabling the community to extend the functionality, making Sonar the one-stop-shop for source code quality by addressing not only the developer's requirements, but also the manager's needs.

Sonar Code Quality Testing Essentials will help you understand the different factors that define code quality and how to improve your own or your team's code using Sonar.

You will learn to use Sonar effectively and explore the quality of your source code on the following axes:

- Coding standards
- Documentation and comments
- Potential bugs and defects
- Unit-testing coverage
- Design and complexity

Through practical examples, you will customize Sonar components and widgets to identify areas where your source code is lacking. The book goes on to propose good practices and common solutions that you can put to use to improve such code.

You will start with installing and setting up a Sonar server and performing your first project analysis. Then you will go through the process of creating a custom and balanced quality profile exploring all Sonar components through practical examples. After reading the book, you will be able to analyze any project using Sonar and know how to read and evaluate quality metrics.

Hunting potential bugs and eliminating complexity are the hottest topics regarding code quality. The book will guide you through the process of finding such problematic areas, leveraging and customizing the most appropriate components. Knowing the best tool for each task is essential.

While you improve code and design through the book, you will notice that metrics go high and alerts turn green. You will use the Time Machine and the Timeline to examine how your changes affected the quality.

Sonar Code Quality Testing Essentials will enable you to perform custom quality analysis on any Java project and quickly gain insight on even large code bases, as well as provide possible solutions to code defects and complexity matters.

What this book covers

Chapter 1, An Overview of Sonar, covers the Sonar quality management platform and its features. It also discusses the different aspects of quality and the role of metrics.

Chapter 2, Installing Sonar, guides you to successfully installing the Sonar platform, and how to perform basic administration tasks such as backing up project data and installing plugins.

Chapter 3, Analyzing Your First Project, walks you through setting up a project for analysis and showcasing the Sonar dashboard. Finally, you will eliminate violations and further reflect on project quality and progression.

Chapter 4, Following Coding Standards, introduces coding standards and Sonar rules. You will learn how to detect coding standards errors and eliminate code violations through practical examples.

Chapter 5, Managing Measures and Getting Feedback, introduces Sonar quality profiles and discusses different development needs and rule sets. Additionally, the reader will learn how to create custom metric alerts and get visual feedback on quality and review historical data.

Chapter 6, Hunting Potential Bugs, covers code violations that can lead to potential software bugs. You will learn how to use Sonar hunting tools to detect such violations following practical examples.

Chapter 7, Refining Your Documentation, teaches how to find undocumented source code. We then discuss documentation practices and documentation-generation tools.

Chapter 8, Working with Duplicated Code, discusses code duplication and guides you on how to spot duplicated code and possible methods to eliminate it.

Chapter 9, Analyzing Complexity and Design, covers how software complexity is presented in Sonar and further discusses complexity metrics. You will get a good grasp of complexity metrics and learn how to identify and review them with Sonar.

Chapter 10, Code Coverage and Testing, covers how Sonar measures code coverage and how it helps in writing cost-effective unit tests covering complexity that matters.

Chapter 11, Integrating Sonar, introduces you to the Continuous Inspection Paradigm and serves as a reference guide on how to set up and enable an integrated build environment providing constant Sonar quality reporting.

Appendix, Sonar Metrics Index, has reference to software metrics supported by Sonar.

What you need for this book

You will need the following software to follow the examples:

- Java JDK 1.6+
- Sonar latest version (http://www.sonarsource.org)
- Eclipse (http://www.eclipse.org)
- Apache Maven build tool (http://maven.apache.org/)
- Apache Ant build tool (http://ant.apache.org/)

Who this book is for

This book is for you if you are a Java developer or a Team Manager familiar with Java and want to ensure the quality of your code using Sonar. You should have a background with Java and unit testing in general. The book follows a step-by-step tutorial enriched with practical examples and the necessary screenshots for easy and quick learning.

Conventions

In this book, you will find a number of styles of text that distinguish between different kinds of information. Here are some examples of these styles, and an explanation of their meaning.

Code words in text are shown as follows: "Open a command prompt and type the telnet command."

A block of code is set as follows:

```
327     if (!Token.containsTokenWithValue(tokens, y) && years != 0) {
                while (years != 0) {
                        months += 12 * years;
                        years = 0;
                }
        }
```

When we wish to draw your attention to a particular part of a code block, the relevant lines or items are set in bold:

```
[INFO]   Database dialect class org.sonar.jpa.dialect.MySql
[INFO]   Initializing Hibernate
[INFO]   ------------ Analyzing Commons Lang 3
[INFO]   Selected quality profile : [name=Sonar way,language=java]
[INFO]   Configure maven plugins...
[INFO]   Compare to previous analysis
[INFO]   Compare over 5 days (2011-11-09)
[INFO]   Compare over 30 days (2011-10-15)
[INFO]   Sensor JavaSourceImporter...
[INFO]   Sensor JavaSourceImporter done: 32279 ms
...
[INFO]   Sensor TrackerSensor done: 1889 ms
[INFO]   Execute decorators...
[INFO]   ANALYSIS SUCCESSFUL, you can browse http://IP_ADDRESS:9000/
sonar
```

Any command-line input or output is written as follows:

```
$ $SONAR_RUNNER_HOME/bin/sonar-runner -h
usage: sonar-runner [options]
Options:
 -h,--help              Display help information
 -X,--debug             Produce execution debug output
 -D,--define <arg>      Define property
```

New terms and important words are shown in bold. Words that you see on the screen, in menus or dialog boxes for example, appear in the text like this: "Select **Add filter** to navigate to filter configuration settings screen".

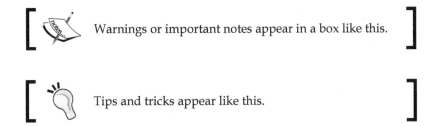

[Warnings or important notes appear in a box like this.]

[Tips and tricks appear like this.]

Reader feedback

Feedback from our readers is always welcome. Let us know what you think about this book—what you liked or may have disliked. Reader feedback is important for us to develop titles that you really get the most out of.

To send us general feedback, simply send an e-mail to feedback@packtpub.com, and mention the book title through the subject of your message.

If there is a topic that you have expertise in and you are interested in either writing or contributing to a book, see our author guide on www.packtpub.com/authors.

Customer support

Now that you are the proud owner of a Packt book, we have a number of things to help you to get the most from your purchase.

Downloading the example code

You can download the example code files for all Packt books you have purchased from your account at http://www.packtpub.com. If you purchased this book elsewhere, you can visit http://www.packtpub.com/support and register to have the files e-mailed directly to you.

Errata

Although we have taken every care to ensure the accuracy of our content, mistakes do happen. If you find a mistake in one of our books — maybe a mistake in the text or the code — we would be grateful if you would report this to us. By doing so, you can save other readers from frustration and help us improve subsequent versions of this book. If you find any errata, please report them by visiting http://www.packtpub.com/support, selecting your book, clicking on the **errata submission form** link, and entering the details of your errata. Once your errata are verified, your submission will be accepted and the errata will be uploaded to our website, or added to any list of existing errata, under the Errata section of that title.

Piracy

Piracy of copyright material on the Internet is an ongoing problem across all media. At Packt, we take the protection of our copyright and licenses very seriously. If you come across any illegal copies of our works, in any form, on the Internet, please provide us with the location address or website name immediately so that we can pursue a remedy.

Please contact us at copyright@packtpub.com with a link to the suspected pirated material.

We appreciate your help in protecting our authors, and our ability to bring you valuable content.

Questions

You can contact us at questions@packtpub.com if you are having a problem with any aspect of the book, and we will do our best to address it.

1
An Overview of Sonar

This chapter provides an overview of Sonar, presenting the objectives and features of the platform, and highlighting how developers and software quality benefit from it. It follows an overview of the platform's architecture, so as to gain a better understanding about how Sonar analyzes and measures quality. Finally, the chapter closes by discussing the Sonar community and its ecosystem. In this chapter we cover:

- What is Sonar?
- Features of Sonar
- Covering software quality on Seven Axes
- Architecture of Sonar
- Source code analyzers
- The Sonar community and ecosystem

What is Sonar

Sonar is a software quality management platform primarily for **Java** programming language, enabling developers to access and track code analysis data ranging from styling errors, potential bugs, and code defects to design inefficiencies, code duplication, lack of test coverage, and excess complexity. Everything that affects our code base, from minor styling details to critical design errors, is inspected and evaluated by Sonar.

Consider Sonar as your team's quality and improvement agent. While the primary supported language is Java, more languages are supported with extensions or commercial plugins, for example C, PHP, and JavaScript. At the time of writing, more than 10 languages were supported with plans to add more in the future. The additional languages are supported in the form of plugins, taking advantage of the platform's extensible and flexible architecture.

How it works

Sonar collects and analyzes source code, measuring quality and providing reports for your projects. It combines static and dynamic analysis tools and enables quality to be measured continuously over time. More than 600 code rules are incorporated into the platform, checking the code from different perspectives.

Rules are separated into different logical groups and each one contributes at a different level towards the overall quality of the project in case. Analysis results, code violations, and historical data are all available and accessible through a well-thought-out user interface consisting of different components, with each one serving and fulfilling different needs and scopes.

The Sonar platform analyzes source code from different aspects. To achieve this, Sonar drills down to your code layer by layer, moving from module level down to class level. Picture this as a vertical movement through your source code from top to bottom components. At each level, Sonar performs both static and dynamic analysis producing metric values and statistics, revealing problematic areas in the source that require inspection or improvement. The analysis is not a monolithic procedure but examines code from different perspectives, introducing the concept of *axes of quality*. The results are then interpreted and consolidated in a very informative and visually appealing dashboard, enabling you to form an opinion about defective code and quality testing over projects. You can now take educated decisions as to where to start fixing things in a cost-effective manner, reducing the technical debt.

Although Sonar can be run as a one-off auditor, where the platform really shines is when you have it track and check your source code continuously. While a single inspection proves to be useful at times, it does not make the most out of the platform. The intended use is to have Sonar integrated into the team's development process, exploiting the platform's true capabilities.

If all these sound complex and advanced, they are not. It is a matter of a single download and running a script to have Sonar up and running, waiting to assess our code. Afterward, we can choose among different methods of how to import projects into the platform for analysis.

What makes Sonar different

What makes Sonar really stand out is that it not only provides metrics and statistics about your code but translates these nondescript values to real business values such as risk and technical debt. This conversion plays a major role in the philosophy of the platform enabling a new business dimension to unfold, which is invaluable to project management. Sonar not only addresses to core developers and programmers but to project managers and even higher managerial levels as well, due to the management aspect it offers. This concept is strengthened more by Sonar's enhanced reporting capabilities and multiple views addressing source code from different perspectives.

From a managerial perspective, transparent and continuous access on historical data enables the manager to ask the right questions.

To better illustrate this, the following are some possible cases discussing quality and source code matters based on feedback from Sonar, either visual or textual:

Case 1: Complexity has jumped up lately; should we further examine the design and implementation of the recently added features? (Notice the line that represents overall complexity increasing close to 9.000.)

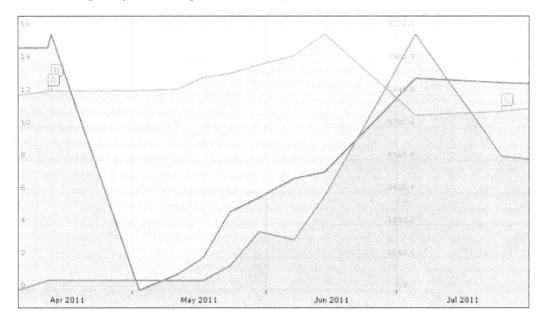

Case 2: Many major violations popped up during the last iteration. Are things moving too fast? Is the team taking more than it can handle? What about pace? (Sonar reports 589 major code violations.)

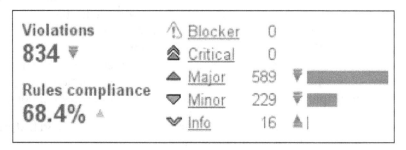

Case 3: Documentation is lacking and team composition is about to change. Let us clarify and better explain what our code is about. At least the public API! (Big red boxes represent undocumented public APIs.)

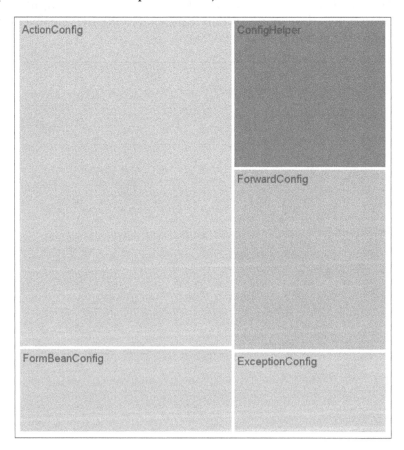

Sonar in the lifecycle

Sonar in the development environment acts as a quality management center. It is the place of reference when code quality matters arise, and sessions with team members drilling down views, exploring deficiencies and discussing software design and its implementation are not uncommon. The ease of the installation process and the broad accessibility by the web interface make it a perfect choice to inspect and share code quality among managers and developers.

An extra step is added to the developers' lifecycle, that of quality review and inspection. After updating and committing code, tests are executed within the context of the build server, producing a fresh artifact. Then, Sonar takes over collecting and analyzing source code and test results. Once the analysis process is complete, the Sonar dashboard is updated with inspection data reflecting the latest changes.

It is vital not to force Sonar into the development process but let the team embrace it.

Let us put technical details and issues aside for a moment and focus more on the psychological aspect of this process as a whole. There is no more rewarding experience for a developer than watching the results of his/her work on a daily basis, experiencing how his/her actions directly reflect upon the improvisation of the final product. Eventually, Sonar proves to be an essential part of a development setup, while the whole process becomes second nature to the developer.

There is one obstacle though that every development team will meet, that of the fear barrier and how to get over it. And by fear, we mean the fear to expose the quality of team members' source code, or most importantly the lack of it. And this is perfectly normal and expected.

Overcoming the fear barrier

What you can do is run Sonar *undercover* for a couple of iterations, touching and bettering only your code, escaping comments and reviews on team members. Another approach would be to use it only as an information tool, without emphasizing it. Once you start writing better code, and have substantially improved and corrected errors, you can then host a team session highlighting the platform, presenting the positive effects upon the project, in an effort to encourage team members to use it for improvisation.

One good point would be to emphasize on how rewarding the experience is to watch quality grow over time in response to code corrections and design changes. This warm feeling is the best incentive for each and every developer.

Features of Sonar

The Sonar platform comes with a vast array of components in order to provide insightful and accurate information. Moreover, its flexible architecture allows functionality to be added on demand via a plugin system.

Let's take a closer look at the features the core platform has to offer:

Overview of all projects

With Sonar's project dashboard, you gain quick access to and insight about all your projects through a comprehensive dashboard. The dashboard presents vital quality metrics in an efficient way, highlights sections which require your attention, and finally includes common interface practicalities, such as sorting, adding, or removing columns to make browsing easier. The majority of the user interface is implemented in AJAX and the transitions between the different views and drilldowns are quick and smooth. Likewise, the components of the platform from simple to more complex ones are very responsive and react in a timely fashion to your actions.

Projects	Activity over 90 days	Open Source Forges	Sonar Platform Activity	Sonar Plugins			

Alert	Name ^	Lines of code	Coverage	SQALE Remediation Cost	Duplicated lines (%)	Build date
	MasterProject	9,499,676	29.1%	89,334.0	7.8%	08 Feb 2012
	ActiveMQ	169,266		1,314.8	23.6%	22 Jan 2012
	Activiti	60,256	41.1%	559.3	6.5%	04 Feb 2012
	Adobe Flex PMD Java Parent	16,696	89.4%	24.3	2.3%	04 Feb 2012
	AisLib application framework	12,187	38.4%	109.0	2.0%	03 Feb 2012
	All Sonar plugins	54,500	59.3%	121.5	3.8%	08 Feb 2012
	Apache Abdera	49,458		257.6	2.9%	03 Feb 2012
	Apache Amber	5,099	32.7%	27.8	1.2%	04 Feb 2012
	Apache Archiva	34,366	55.1%	203.7	6.4%	22 Jan 2012
	Apache Aries	49,209	38.6%	496.4	3.1%	19 Mar 2011
	Apache Asyncweb Parent	9,640	34.4%	89.6	2.9%	04 Feb 2012
	Apache Cocoon 3: Root	19,995	32.9%	155.7	1.5%	03 Feb 2012
	Apache Commons Digester	9,917	71.2%	49.9	3.9%	04 Feb 2012
	Apache Commons OGNL - Object Graph Navigation Library	13,417	69.7%	82.5	13.0%	04 Feb 2012
	Apache CXF	236,628	38.7%	2,597.2	5.3%	04 Feb 2012
	Apache Directory Complete Build With All Projects	385,355	20.3%		11.4%	22 Oct 2011
	Apache Empire-db	32,313	13.9%	374.1	10.1%	03 Feb 2012
	Apache Felix	170,782	10.9%	2,423.8	2.4%	27 Aug 2011
	Apache Hama parent POM	14,367	45.8%	142.1	0.6%	04 Feb 2012

The dashboard is fully customizable, and you can select which metric columns each view contains and reorder them as you like. The ability to internationalize the platform is a huge plus allowing you to present a total solution covering every aspect, from pleasant and practical interface to language settings. Generally speaking, language friendliness is very much welcomed if you intend to provide a Sonar instance to a less-technical audience.

If you want to take look at the Sonar dashboard in full swing, point your browser at Nemo, a Sonar demo instance by SonarSource S.A. hosting the platform's own source code among other well-known open source projects at `http://nemo.sonarsource.org`.

Coding rules

More than 600 rules are incorporated into Sonar, performing simple checks to complex calculations. Rules can be fully parameterized to meet different development needs, and if this is not enough, with a little help from the lively community, you can even implement your own, covering every possible need.

The strictest Sonar profile includes about 720 rules, but probably you won't ever need to activate it. It is not even suggested to use all of them at all. The objective is to provide as many coding rules as possible and let the developer make choices accordingly, assigning them to custom profiles for projects. Obviously, there is the ability to host multiple different profiles with specific sets of rules and further assign these profiles to different projects for maximum flexibility.

Standard software metrics

Metrics are necessary to form objective and reliable opinion on any piece of software. Like in every science or process, metrics are essential to measure and reproduce behavior and functionality, and help evaluate/compare source code, establishing a common ground among different pieces of software. In other words, metrics form a common denominator for all software and they have become an integral part of the development process.

Not a magic bullet

Sonar is not a magic bullet. A solid development process, creativity, dedication, and practical design are still some of the necessary virtues to create a successful and quality product. Writing code for the sake of metrics is basically cheating. Tricking the system to produce desirable results, disconnected from the functional requirements, is as you understand under-productive. Such a bad practice only detracts from the final product instead of improving it.

One use for software metrics, which does not have to do directly with quality is that they can also provide insight and deeper knowledge about the source code, revealing potential pitfalls, and providing a safe guideline for new developers to follow. Sonar includes all classical metrics related to software development, some of them being:

- Lines of code
- Documented API
- Cyclomatic complexity
- Test coverage
- Duplicated code

Unit tests

If you have at least a couple of development years under your belt at some time or another, you have probably wondered how you could ever manage without writing any tests for your code. Untested software results in an unstable product, not working as expected. Experience shows that the first thing the end user does with an untested feature ends up to be unexpected and never taken into consideration during development. Random input, experimenting, or using the feature/component for something other than what it was designed for, are all viable and very real cases. While clients demand dynamic help systems and comprehensive manuals, they never ever read them, expecting the software to meet their expectations one way or another.

Software testing verifies that a feature will work as expected and meets design requirements. However, writing tests for the sake of testing only to cheat the metrics, covering low-risk code, and leaving out crucial areas, is pointless. This kind of testing, while it consumes time and resources, adds nothing to the final quality of your product.

Sonar identifies high-risk software pieces and locates untested code not only at line, but even at branch level, taking into consideration all possible outcomes of a conditional operation. Additionally, Sonar provides useful statistics concerning test successes and total duration.

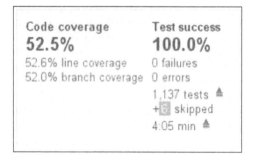

Drill down to source code

Knowing where quality suffers and what aspects of your software need to be strengthened is one thing, specifically locating these problematic areas is another. Sonar features smart components as the metrics radiator that in combination with the dashboard allow you to drill down effortlessly to your source code reaching classes that require attention quickly. It may sound like a complex investigative task or an alternative search tool for your source code but this is not the case.

Drill down is a standard professional method used to browse code. You set a focal point, undocumented code for example, and move downwards from summary information to more detailed data, subsequently exploring modules, packages, and classes.

Time Machine

Sonar stores all analysis results in a database, preserving historical data for future reference and comparison, enabling you to track the evolution of your code. At any time you can check out a past version of your codebase from the repository and add it to the project's time line for comparison. Examining a data point in isolation can enlighten your team about the state of the code in the given time frame, but the information accumulated by the historical data proves to be invaluable in the long run, helping to determine the best approach for the health of your project.

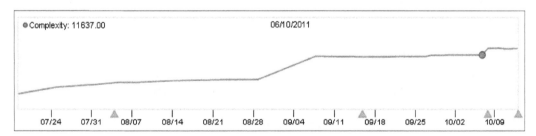

You can examine the progress of your code using one of the three different components available: the *Time Machine*, the *Motion Chart*, and the *Timeline*. Each component can be dynamically customized to access historical data on all metrics supported. The *Motion Chart*, the fanciest of the components, features an animated bubble chart tracking metrics in four different dimensions: the X and Y axes, plus the color and size of the bubbles.

Maven ready

Maven is a build automation tool like Ant, streamlining the steps of the build process in software development. Checking out code, compiling, generating documentation and reports, running tests, producing artifacts, and finally deploying them, are some of the goals supported by Maven and implemented via plugins. Different profiles described in XML configuration files dictate the execution steps that take place during the build process while providing configuration details.

The Sonar platform takes advantage of the Maven goal-oriented philosophy, simplifying configuration. All you have to do is add the *Sonar Maven Plugin* into your project to get support for Sonar-oriented goals. The only requirement is to have the Sonar server up whenever the goal is executed. Basically, the setup requires zero or minimal configuration if you are familiar with Maven.

User friendly

Much thought and work has been put into the platform's user interface in regards to both appearance and behavior. The clean interface is mostly self-explanatory but if you have any queries or feel like clarifying some things more, there is plenty of documentation and media available within the Sonar community covering many topics, from traditional getting started wikis to screencasts exploring advanced Sonar features. It is important to note here the web nature of the user interface, accessible straight from your browser.

Unified components

Sonar introduces a new paradigm on measuring quality without trying to reinvent the wheel in the field of metrics and rules. While it features its own implemented set of rules, under the hood most work is handled by familiar and long-trusted tools. Sonar unifies these tools, leveraging existing functionality, collecting output, and finally refining the results to follow suit with the platform's objective.

As SonarSource puts it:

> *Sonar can transparently orchestrate all those components for you.*

Obviously, the procedure of running these tools manually in sequence to produce raw values and statistics is now rendered obsolete, since Sonar automatically streams the whole process in one combined analysis step.

Security measures

Sonar features a standard role-based authentication system allowing you to secure your instance, create as many users as required, and assign them to groups. A user can belong to more than one group, while access to the various Sonar services and functionality can be fine-grained by assigning appropriate roles.

Two groups have a special status in Sonar:

- **Anyone**: is a group that exists in the system but cannot be managed. Every user belongs to this group.
- **Sonar-users**: is the default group to which every user exists. It is not possible to configure the name of this group.

Of the four roles available in Sonar, one is global, referring to the instance, and the three others are attached to projects:

- **Global Administrators**: Can perform all administration functions for the instance: global configuration, personalization of the Time Machine, and the home page
- **Project Administrators**: Can perform administration functions for a project by accessing its settings
- **Project Users**: Can navigate through every service of a project, except viewing source code and settings
- **Project Code Viewers**: Can view the source code of a project

If a global security system exists within your environment, such as Atlassian Crowd SSO, LDAP, or Microsoft Active Directory, you can delegate all Sonar authentication function to these systems using the appropriate plugins.

Extensible plugin system

The Sonar platform is extensible via a plugin system. More functionality can be added using plugins, either open source or commercial. A dedicated repository located at `http://sonar-plugins.codehaus.org/` hosts the Sonar plugin library. From there, you can choose and download the plugins you require for your Sonar instance and read documentation and installation instructions specifically written for each one separately. Plugins enable Sonar to measure more programming languages, add more metrics and rules, and integrate the platform with third-party systems such as LDAP or Continuous Integration build servers.

Some of the more interesting plugins and a brief description of what they do are shown in the following list:

- Additional languages:
    - *PHP*: Analysis using PHP Unit, PHP Depend, PHP MD, and SQLI CodeSniffer
    - *Groovy*
    - *JavaScript*
    - *C, C#*
    - *Web*: currently supports analysis for JSF and JSP pages.

- Additional metrics:
    - Build stability: Reports on stability of project build using Continuous Integration engine data
    - Rules meter: Gives information on the level of activation of projects' quality profiles
    - Sonargraph: Provides architecture governance features accompanied by metrics about cyclic dependencies and other structural aspects
    - Useless code: Reports on the number of lines that can be reduced in an application

- Visualization/Reporting:
    - PDF Report: Generates a PDF report with analysis results
    - Timeline: Displays measures history using a Google Timeline Chart to replay the past

- Governance:
    - Quality Index: Calculates a global Quality Index based on coding rules, style, complexity, and unit-testing coverage
    - Technical debt: Calculates the technical debt on every component with breakdown by duplications, documentation, coverage, and complexity
    - SQALE – Quality Model (Commercial): An implementation of the SQALE Methodology

- Integration:
  - ° Hudson/Jenkins and Bamboo: Enables to configure and launch Sonar analysis from Hudson or Jenkins continuous integration engines
  - ° Crowd and LDAP: Enables delegation of Sonar authentication to Atlassian Crowd and to LDAP or Microsoft Active Directory respectively
  - ° Switch off violations: Excludes some violations in a fine-grained way

- IDE:
  - ° Eclipse: Accesses information gathered by Sonar directly in Eclipse and fixes them on the spot

- Localization:
  - ° Supports French and Spanish languages

Covering software quality on Seven Axes

First of all, it is important to point out that quality is a perceptional concept and quite subjective. One way to define software quality is through abstractions and examining it from different perspectives.

Take a moment to read the following lines:

I cdnuolt blveiee taht I cluod aculaclty uesdnatnrd waht I was rdgnieg. The phaonmneal pweor of the hmuan mnid. It deosn't mttaer in waht oredr the leteerrs in a wrod are, the olny iprmoatnt tihng is taht the frist and lsat ltteer be in the rghit pclae. The rset can be a taotl msess and you can sitll raed it wouthit a porbelm. Tihs is bcuseae the huamn mnid deos not raed ervey lteter by istlef, but the wrod as a wlohe.

The preceding text does not contain one single word spelled correctly but proves to be readable. The preceding paragraph tests the human brain's ability to recognize common patterns rather than convey a message to the reader. From a product perspective, someone could support that although the text is flawed it does the job, since it manages to remain understandable. But this has the side effect of deteriorating the final reading experience, requiring additional effort to reconstruct the words and phrases. The reader unconsciously stresses his mind in an effort to adapt and decipher the messed-up words, sharing focus between restructuring text, and understanding what is actually written, a not-so-pleasant user experience. On the other hand, the editor assigned to improve or add to the text would have to cope with this non-standard writing practice delaying the whole process.

Switch the corrupt text for a software product's source code. The reader is now the end user of the product and the editor the developer. They both experience product quality differently, each one from their own views. The end user from a functional perspective while the developer from a structural one.

Generally speaking, it is common to separate quality into:

- **External quality** — assures that the product obeys to the functional requirements/specifications
- **Internal quality** — assures that the software's structure supports the delivery of the functional requirements

To measure external quality the product is treated like a *black box*, testing and interacting its exposed features, observing behavior, and reassuring that it works as expected according to the requirements.

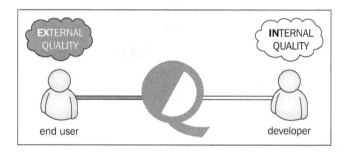

To measure internal quality, esoteric inspection of the software is required. The structure of the source code is analyzed and evaluated against coding standards and practices. As for software design, it is necessary to examine at what level it adheres to basic principles of software architecture. This approach of measuring quality is referred to as a **white box approach** because it deals with the software's internal workings, peeking inside source code. The Sonar platform does exactly that, measuring the internal quality of a software piece. However, it is important to note that high internal quality does not enforce or guarantee external quality, but it indirectly betters it in terms of its overall outcome.

How Sonar manages quality

Software quality measurement is a quantitative process summing up weighted attribute values, which in part describe specific software characteristics. For each characteristic, a set of such measurable attributes is defined, and the existence of such characteristic, or its quality factor, is directly correlated to those attributes.

As a matter of fact, quality is rated along many different dimensions. Likewise, Sonar classifies associated attributes and metrics in seven dimensions, seven technical axes of quality which the Sonar team prefers to cal them as:

> *The seven deadly sins of a developer.*

Overall, Sonar defines the following technical axes:

- Coding standards — respect coding standards and follow best practices
- Potential bugs — eliminate code violations to prevent vulnerabilities
- Documentation and comments — provide documentation especially for the *Public API*, the source code
- Duplicated code — isolates and refines duplications, *Don't Repeat Yourself*
- Complexity — equalizes disproportionate distributed complexity among components; eliminates complexity if possible
- Test coverage — writes unit tests, especially for complex parts of the software
- Design and architecture — minimize dependencies

DRY — Don't Repeat Yourself

Don't Repeat Yourself is a programming principle aimed at reducing repetition of code. The DRY principle is stated as:

Every piece of knowledge must have a single, unambiguous, authoritative representation within a system.

Source code written with this principle in mind is obviously easier to maintain. When a bug arises, there is only one single point in the source responsible for the malfunction and patching this point would suffice, without the need to modify other parts of the software.

Architecture of Sonar

The core engine of the platform, *Squid*, is supported by additional code analyzers which Sonar orchestrates together to measure quality.

The following diagram represents the upper-level components of the platform and how they interact with each other:

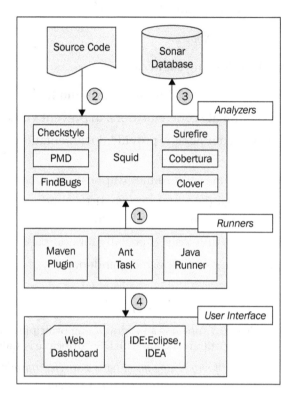

1. An analysis request is triggered using one of three possible methods:
    -   Maven Plugin
    -   Ant Task
    -   Java Runner

2. Sonar receives the request and starts analyzing the project's source code. The analysis is based on the project's Sonar profile activating any additional plugins or reporting capabilities, if any.

3. When the analysis is over, results are stored to a database for future reference and history tracking.

4. Finally, the user interface and its components are updated with the new data. You can access data from your browser and the web dashboard. Conveniently, Sonar reporting is also made available within your IDE, either Eclipse or IDEA, allowing you to review and correct code violations on the spot.

In a continuously integrated environment, the analysis process is triggered by the build server. The server checks out source code from the repository, compiles and executes all unit or integration tests, after which it produces the necessary builds. Finally, Sonar takes over analyzing the source. A good practice for a time-consuming process such as this is to trigger it once a day, when developers are inactive. The process is then called a **nightly job** and the final build produced a **nightly snapshot**. Next time, developers will have access to the latest data and reports about the project, enabling them to review how recent changes affected the overall quality of the project.

Source code analyzers

To analyze code, Sonar utilizes some of the most popular and proven tools available in the open source community. These tools pass through source code performing standard checks reviewing errors and possible bugs, each from their own perspective. The nature of the checks range from minor styling ones, for example the detection of unwanted trailing spaces, to more complex ones that easily promote to potential bugs, such as unchecked variables eligible to result in null references. Since version 2.1 Sonar provides its own rules engine too, based on Squid.

Sonar includes the following five analyzers:

*   Squid — `http://docs.codehaus.org/display/SONAR/Documentation`
*   Checkstyle — `http://checkstyle.sourceforge.net/`
*   PMD — `http://pmd.sourceforge.net/`
*   FindBugs — `http://findbugs.sourceforge.net/`
*   Cobertura — `http://cobertura.sourceforge.net/`
*   Clover — `http://www.atlassian.com/software/clover/`

Squid

Sonar's core analyzer Squid, works on Java dependencies and calculates object-oriented metrics. It implements the visitor pattern to visit dependencies between methods, fields, classes, and packages. Some of the metrics calculated are the following:

*   RFC — Response for Class
*   LCOM4 — Lack of Cohesion Methods
*   DIT — Depth of Inheritance Tree
*   NOC — Number of Children

Checkstyle

Checkstyle ensures that all source code adheres to coding standards. Its main duty is to check code from an aesthetic perspective with emphasis on layout and styling. However, during its development more checks were added straying away from the initial coding style and standards concept. Now Checkstyle is capable of performing broader checks like identifying class design problems, duplication, and common bug patterns. Checkstlyle, and the rest of the tools we are going to examine here, can also run standalone.

Bug patterns

A **bug pattern** is badly structured code that under certain circumstances can produce errors. These vulnerabilities may not always fail a test case but can potentially lead to memory outage, performance degradation, security breaches, and many other problems. Such common error-prone structures have been identified and standardized, so that they can be identified easily by source code analyzers.

PMD

According to its creator, a standard definition for the PMD acronym does not exist. In any case, the following are some interpretations taken straight away from the *What does it mean* section of the project 's SourceForge page:

Project Mess Detector

Programs of Mass Destruction

Project Meets Deadline

Head on to PMD's home page for a more comprehensive list.

PMD scans Java source code and reports on problems such as the following:

- Possible bugs — empty / try / catch / finally / switch statements
- Dead code — unused local variables, parameters, and private methods
- Suboptimal code — wasteful String / StringBuffer code
- Complex expressions — unnecessary if statements, for loops instead of while
- Duplicate code — copied/ pasted code

FindBugs

FindBugs performs static analysis to check source code and trace bugs and defects. It covers many different aspects such as vulnerabilities, malicious code, performance, and coding standards.

Cobertura and Clover

Cobertura, based on the *jcoverage* Java library, is used to calculate the percentage of code accessed by tests and identify which parts of your source code lack test coverage. Additionally, it calculates cyclomatic complexity for each class and the average cyclomatic complexity for each package.

Clover emphasizes more on test coverage, providing a rich user interface and can be easily used as a standalone tool, offering a complete quality testing solution.

The Sonar community and ecosystem

Sonar, like every respectable open source project, comes with a thriving community and a vibrant ecosystem built around it.

The community features four separate mailing lists to discuss everything Sonar:

- scm@sonar.codehaus.org
- user@sonar.codehaus.org
- dev@sonar.codehaus.org
- announce@sonar.codehaus.org

A dedicated issue tracker to track Sonar development and submit tickets can be found at the following URL:

http://jira.codehaus.org/browse/SONAR

A comprehensive documentation wiki maintained by Sonar's team members can be found at:

http://docs.codehaus.org/display/SONAR/Documentation

The official Sonar blog can be found at:

http://www.sonarsource.org/category/blog/

Additionally, Sonar has a strong presence across social networks:

- Linkedin: `http://www.linkedin.com/company/sonarsource/products`
- Twitter: `@SonarSource`

If you want to learn more about Sonar or even write your own plugins for the platform, Sonar's plugin ecosystem in combination with a friendly and welcoming community provides everything you will need.

You can subscribe to the developers' list, request access to Sonar's source control management system Forge, and benefit from the continuous integration environment that has been set up to serve development needs by navigating to the following URL:

- Forge: `http://www.sonarsource.org/forge/`

The SonarSource company

Sonar was founded in 2008 by SonarSource S.A., a Swiss company that brought forth a bold statement:

> *SonarSource S.A.: democratize access to software quality management*
>
> `http://www.sonarsource.com/`

Thus Sonar was born, in an effort to fulfill the company's objective to create a platform that would enable easy and continuous access to code quality metrics. The big picture was the platform to achieve such high adoption rates, capable of establishing it as a commodity in development teams along with IDEs.

The company did not only succeed, but pushed things further with the introduction of the **Continuous Inspection** paradigm similar to the Continuous Integration practices, a movement that is now considered to be a best practice among development teams and members especially in the context of an agile environment.

The SonarSource team:

- CEO and Founder at SonarSource: Olivier Gaudin `@gaudol`
- Co-Founder and Product Manager: Freddy Mallet `@FreddyMallet`
- Co-Founder and Technical Lead: Simon Brandhof `@SimonBrandhof`
- Software Gardener: Evgeny Mandrikov `@_godin_`
- Product Manager: Fabrice Bellingar `@bellingard`

Awards and conferences

SonarSource, since its inception has jolted the software industry, creating an innovative platform that caused significant impact as long as quality management is considered. In comparison to other tools, the Sonar platform was revolutionary, inventing a new method towards quality inspection, which later became a standard practice under the term Continuous Inspection. Therefore, in 2010 it received the Jolt Productivity Award for providing a manager's best friend with highlights on the detailed dashboard, the tracking of historical data, and code analysis from different perspectives.

After initial versions of the platform were publicly released, Sonar was presented at numerous JavaOne conferences and was recommended as the tool of choice to measure, track, and gain access to code quality data. In most cases, the platform was sitting next to a Hudson/Jenkins build server in a continuous integration setup.

Sonar license

The Sonar platform is open source and distributed under the **GNU Lesser General Public License Version 3**, the most widely used license for free software. This means that you can modify and redistribute the platform freely as long as all software and modifications released still remain under the GPL Version 3.

Apart from the core platform and the free plugins developed and gardened by the community, SonarSource company offers commercial products built around the extensible Sonar ecosystem. Worth mentioning is the **SQALE** plugin, a full implementation of the Software Quality Assessment method based on Lifecycle Expectations. If you want to learn more about this method you can point your browser at `http://www.sonarsource.com` and navigate from there to the plugins section.

Additionally, among other services, SonarSource company offers professional support carried out by Sonar's core contributors and accepts requests to develop plugins on demand in case additional functionality is required.

Summary

This chapter gave an overview of the Sonar platform, its history, and its features. We further explored the concept of quality in software products and how it is measured.

We analyzed the methodology of covering quality on seven axes and detailed the Sonar architecture along with the code analyzers it provides. Finally, we took a closer look around the Sonar community and its ecosystem.

In the next chapter, we will focus on setting up the environment and installing Sonar along with plugins.

2
Installing Sonar

In this chapter, we will install Sonar along with required software in either Linux or Windows. We will need to install MySQL, create a new database to store Sonar data, install Maven to import projects easily into Sonar, configure it to run as a service, and finally secure our instance by creating groups and users. Then, we will go through the process of installing plugins, updating Sonar from the update center, and backing up our data.

In this chapter we will cover:

- Prerequisites for Sonar
- Installing the Sonar web server
- Configuring MySQL
- Starting Sonar as a service
- Logging in to Sonar for the first time
- Securing your Sonar instance
- Creating users and groups
- Backing up your data
- Extending Sonar with plugins
- Upgrading Sonar

Prerequisites for Sonar

Before installing Sonar, it is necessary to check that our host system meets all the requirements.

Sonar comes bundled with the Apache Derby database, but it is highly recommended to use an enterprise database, especially when deploying on to a production environment. A minimum of 512 MB of RAM and sufficient data space to store Sonar's analysis results and historical data are required. The last requirement should not be an issue since the public Nemo instance of Sonar uses 4 GB of RAM to analyze more than 6 million lines of code within a two-year lifespan according to SonarSource. Users will interact with Sonar through web browsers and it is recommended to enable JavaScript if not already enabled. Finally, installing the Maven project builder is highly recommended to make the process of adding new projects for analysis much easier.

The following list presents all supported platforms by Sonar:

- **Java Oracle JDK**
    - 1.5
    - 1.6
    - 1.7 (not tested yet)

- **Database**
    - Microsoft SQL Server 2005
    - MySQL 5.x and 6.x
    - Oracle 10g, 11g, and XE Editions
    - PostgreSQL 8.3, 8.4, 9.0, and 9.1

- **Applications servers**
    - Jetty 6 (bundled with Sonar)
    - Apache Tomcat 5.5, 6.0, and 7.0 (has not been tested yet)

- **Web browsers**
    - Microsoft IE 7 and 8 — Sonar v. 2.12 will fully support IE 9.0
    - Mozilla Firefox (all versions)
    - Google Chrome (latest stable version 12 supported)
    - Safari (latest stable version supported)
    - Opera (not tested)

- **Build runners**
    - ° Maven 2+
    - ° Ant
    - ° Java Runner

Before moving on, let's make sure that Java, Maven, and MySQL are properly installed and configured. We will adopt the following setup:

- Java 1.6
- MySQL 5
- Maven 3.0.3

Checking your Java installation

To check your Java installation, open up a terminal or a command prompt if you are in Windows and enter the following command:

```
$ java -version
```

If Java is installed and correctly configured, the output will be something like this:

```
Java version "1.6.0_26"
Java(TM) SE Runtime Environment (build 1.6.0_26-b03)
Java HotSpot(TM) Server VM (build 20.1-b02, mixed mode)
```

If is not installed, visit Oracle's official website and follow the installation instructions for your system (http://www.java.com/en/download/manual.jsp).

After the installation process is complete, we have to set the JAVA_HOME system variable. In Linux, edit the .bashrc or .bash_profile configuration files, and append the following lines and substitute the path highlighted in the following snippet with yours:

```
# Java Home
export JAVA_HOME=/usr/lib/jvm/java-6-sun-1.6.0.26
export PATH=$JAVA_HOME/bin:$PATH
```

Next, for the changes to take place, we have to reload the configuration files by typing the following command:

```
$ source ~/.bashrc
```

Installing Maven on Linux

Download Maven from `http://maven.apache.org/download.html` and unzip it. Next, the `M2_HOME` variable has to be set. Edit `.bashrc` or `.bash_profile`, and append the following lines and replace the path highlighted in the following code snippet with yours:

```
# Maven Home
export M2_HOME=/usr/local//apache-maven-3.0.3
export PATH=$M2_HOME/bin:$PATH
```

Again, reload the configuration files by using the following command:

```
$ source ~/.bashrc
```

Then, verify the installation by entering the following command:

```
$ mvn -version
```

If everything is done right, the console should show output something like this:

```
Apache Maven 3.0.3 (r1075438; 2011-02-15 19:31:09+0200)
Maven home: /usr/local/apache-maven-3.0.3
Java version: 1.6.0_26, vendor: Sun Microsystems Inc.
Java home: /usr/lib/jvm/java-6-sun-1.6.0.26/jre
Default locale: en_US, platform encoding: UTF-8
OS name: "linux", version: "2.6.32-5-686", arch: "i386", family:
"unix"
```

Installing Maven on Windows

The installation process in Windows is exactly the same as in Linux, with one difference. In Windows, we create the environment variables `JAVA_HOME` and `M2_HOME`, and add them to the Windows system `PATH` variable, using the **Environment Variables** user interface. To verify that the variables are set, open a command prompt and type:

```
> echo %JAVA_HOME%
> echo %M2_HOME%
```

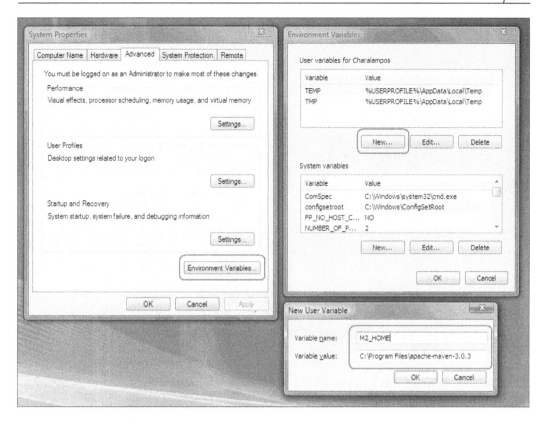

Installing MySQL on Linux

To install MySQL on a Debian or Ubuntu-based Linux distribution, open a terminal and enter the following command:

```
$ apt-get install mysql-client-5.1 mysql-server-5.1
```

When the installation process finishes, the MySQL service starts automatically. You can start/stop the service with the following command:

```
$ service mysql [start|stop]
```

To install for Red Hat distributions such as Fedora or CentOS, open a terminal and enter the following yum command as root:

```
# yum install mysql mysql-server
```

You can start/stop the service with the following command:

```
# service mysqld [start|stop]
```

To create a root account with the MySQL admin utility, enter the following command, substituting `password` with one of your choice:

```
# mysqladmin -u root -p password
```

To connect to the MySQL Server, type the following command, and enter the root password when prompted:

```
$ mysql -u root -p
```

To check the version of the MySQL Server install, use the MySQL command with the `version` switch:

```
$ mysql -version
mysql  Ver 14.14 Distrib 5.1.49, for debian-linux-gnu (i486) using
readline 6.1
```

Installing MySQL on Windows

On Windows, download the MSI installer for the MySQL Community Server from `http://dev.mysql.com/downloads/mysql/` and double-click on the `msi` or `exe` file to start the installation process. An installation wizard will guide you through the process of creating a new MySQL service and a root account. The official MySQL website provides comprehensive documentation and detailed installation guides for all operating systems, just in case.

Downloading Sonar

Sonar is updated frequently, with each release packing a couple of new features and improvements. Visit `http://www.sonarsource.org/downloads/` to get an overview of the releases and download links. From there download the latest version—notice that whether you are on Linux or Windows, the download is the same, since Sonar is based on Java and it is compatible with both. All downloads are `zip` archives named after Sonar's version following this convention:

`sonar-x.yy..zip`, where x is the major release number and `yy` is the minor one.

As of October 15, 2011, the latest version was 2.11 and about 60 MB in size. For the needs of this book, we will go with Sonar v. 2.11.

After the download is complete, extract the `zip` archive into a directory of our choice. It is a good practice to create a `servers` directory and extract Sonar in there. An exemplary directory setup could be `/development/servers/sonar-2.11/`.

Do not unzip Sonar into a directory starting with a digit.]

Installing the Sonar web server

Place the downloaded file in the directory to which you want to install Sonar, open the terminal window, and enter the following command to unzip it:

```
$ unzip sonar-2.11.zip
```

Important Sonar directories to take a note of are:

- `conf`: Sonar, database, and logging configuration in the form of XML and property files are stored here.
- `extensions`: JDBC drivers and Sonar plugins are located here.
- `logs`: All logging goes to this directory; this is the place to check when something goes wrong with our Sonar instance.
- `bin`: This directory contains Sonar startup scripts for different Windows and Linux platforms.

To start the Sonar server in Linux, open a terminal, navigate in to the `bin` directory, and execute the startup script for your platform. For example:

```
$ bin/linux-x86-32/sonar.sh console
```

On Windows 32-bit, execute the following command:

```
$ bin\windows-x86-32\StartSonar.bat
```

When Sonar starts for the first time, it creates and populates the embedded Apache Derby database, so it is natural for it to take a while. This is what the `logs/sonar.log` file looks like after Sonar has been started successfully:

```
INFO  org.sonar.INFO  Enable profiles...
INFO  org.sonar.INFO  Enable profiles done: 40 ms
INFO  org.sonar.INFO  Activate default profile for java
INFO  org.sonar.INFO  Register quality models...
INFO  org.sonar.INFO  Register quality models done: 0 ms
INFO  org.sonar.INFO  Start services done: 14641 ms
INFO  org.sonar.INFO  Sonar started: http://0.0.0.0:9000/
```

Open a browser and go at `http://localhost:9000/` to take a first look at the Sonar dashboard. To stop the Sonar server type, execute the following command:

```
$ bin/linux-x86-32/sonar.sh stop
```

Alternatively, you can press *Ctrl + C* in the console/terminal, to make the Sonar server exit gracefully:

Notice that, if you close the command-line window, the server will stop.

Sonar server basic configuration

The Sonar server listens at port 9000 and binds to all network interfaces 0.0.0.0. The context path is /.To change these settings, edit the `conf/sonar.properties` configuration file accordingly. Open it with an editor and look for the WEB SETTINGS section inside the file. To have the server listening at port 80 under the context `sonar/` and bound at 192.168.1.1, make the following edits:

```
#-----------------------------------------------------------
# WEB SETTINGS - STANDALONE MODE ONLY
# These settings are ignored when the war file is deployed to a JEE
server.
#-----------------------------------------------------------
# Listen host/port and context path (for example / or /sonar). Default
values are 0.0.0.0:9000/.
#sonar.web.host:                        192.168.1.1
sonar.web.port:                         80
sonar.web.context:                      sonar/
```

Sonar can be run inside a J2EE server and deployed as any other web application. To do this, browse into Sonar's war directory and execute build-war.sh or build-war.bat on Windows to create the Sonar server war application. Afterwards, deploy the sonar.war file to the application server. Notice that when deploying to an application server, the Sonar home directory is still needed to store data and host plugins. Thus, the application server must have read/write access to this directory.

Configuring MySQL

While the embedded Apache Derby database is ideal for tests, in a production development environment it is recommended to switch to an enterprise database.

Creating the database

Sonar comes bundled with an SQL script to create the database and the sonar user with the password sonar. The script is located at @SONAR_HOME/extras/database/mysql/create_database.sql. To execute the script, open up a terminal and execute the following command, (enter your root password or sonar when prompted):

```
$ mysql -u root -p < create_database.sql
```

The script creates a new Sonar database with UTF8 encoding and user sonar with password sonar.

Setting up Sonar with MySQL

Having the database up and running, we then must deactivate the embedded Apache Derby and enable MySQL in the conf/sonar.properties configuration file. Stop the server if running, and comment the following lines to disable Apache Derby:

```
# Comment the following lines to deactivate the default embedded
database.
# sonar.jdbc.url:            jdbc:derby://localhost:1527/
sonar;create=true
# sonar.jdbc.driverClassName:       org.apache.derby.jdbc.
ClientDriver
#sonar.jdbc.validationQuery:  values(1)
```

Find the MySQL configuration section in the same file and uncomment the following lines to enable MySQL:

```
#----- MySQL 5.x/6.x
# Comment the embedded database and uncomment the following
#properties to use MySQL. The validation query is optional.
sonar.jdbc.url:jdbc:mysql://localhost:3306/sonar?
    useUnicode=true&characterEncoding=utf8
sonar.jdbc.driverClassName:      com.mysql.jdbc.Driver
sonar.jdbc.validationQuery:          select 1
```

Next time the sever launches, it will establish connection to the MySQL sonar database as user sonar/sonar and create all required tables.

Wait for the MySQL database to initialize, and enter the following commands in a terminal to view the tables created (when asked for your password enter sonar):

```
$ mysqlshow sonar -u sonar -p
+---------------------------+
|           Tables          |
+---------------------------+
| active_dashboards
| active_filters
| active_rule_changes
| active_rule_param_changes
| active_rule_parameters
| ...
```

Starting Sonar as a service

It is most convenient to have the Sonar server start automatically at each boot time. Thus, the final step of the setup is to have it installed as a service.

Run as a service on Linux

Create the file /etc/init.d/sonar with the Vim or Nano editor:

```
sudo nano /etc/init.d/sonar
```

Append the following lines and save it:

```
#! /bin/sh
/usr/bin/sonar $*
```

Open a terminal and enter the following commands:

```
sudo ln -s /home/user/development/servers/sonar-2.11/bin/linux-x86-32/
sonar.sh /usr/bin/sonar
```

```
sudo chmod 755 /etc/init.d/sonar
```

```
sudo update-rc.d sonar defaults
```

Reboot, open a browser, and go to `http://localhost:9000/` to verify that the server is running.

Run as a service on Windows

To install or uninstall the Windows service, simply execute one of the following scripts as administrator respectively:

- **To install**:

  ```
  $ SONAR_HOME/bin/windows-x86-32/InstallNTService.bat
  ```

- **To uninstall**:

  ```
  $ SONAR_HOME/bin/windows-x86-32/UninstallNTService.bat
  ```

You can start/stop the service from Windows Services Administration or execute the start/stop scripts bundled with Sonar:

- **To start**:

  ```
  $ SONAR_HOME/bin/windows-x86-32/StartNTService.bat
  ```

- **To stop**:

  ```
  $ SONAR_HOME/bin/windows-x86-32/StopNTService.bat
  ```

If you experience problems in starting the service due to the missing directory `C:\Windows\system32\config\systemprofile\AppData\Local\Temp\` in Windows 7, create it manually and restart the service.

Logging in to Sonar for the first time

After a fresh reboot, it is finally time to log in to Sonar as an administrator. One of the first things that you should do is change the administrator's credentials.

 Sonar, by default, creates an Administrator account with username `admin` and password `admin`.

Point your browser at `http://localhost:9000/`. At the top right of the dashboard, click on the **Log in** link and fill in the form with username as `admin` and password as `admin`.

To change the default password, click on the **Administrator** link on top and then on **My Profile** on the left. Fill in the **Change Password** form and click on the **Change Password** button to save the changes:

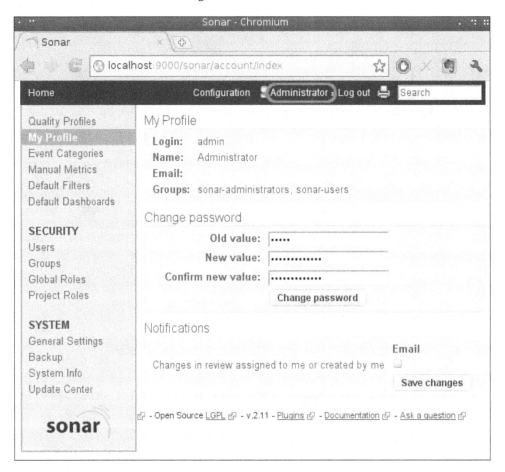

Securing your Sonar instance

In an enterprise environment, a good practice would be to limit access to administration settings and project analysis data according to different members' responsibilities. Administrators should have access to everything, project managers and developers to projects they belong to, while public users could be further limited by preventing them from browsing source code.

Apart from Sonar's standard authentication mechanism, delegation to third-party systems is possible with the use of plugins. If a configured Active Directory or Atlassian's JIRA Crowd Single Sign On solution is already available, you might be interested in the following plugins, which leverage authentication functionality of the aforementioned systems:

- **LDAP plugin**: `http://docs.codehaus.org/display/SONAR/LDAP+Plugin`
- **Crowd plugin**: `http://docs.codehaus.org/display/SONAR/Crowd+Plugin`

Sonar authentication and sources visibility

First of all, you have to configure the level of security for your Sonar instance. By default, the instance is accessible without any authentication. To force user authentication, browse to **Configuration | SYSTEM:General Settings | Security** and set the **Force user authentication** property to **true**:

From now on, each time a user browses to `http://localhost:9000`, he/she will be prompted to fill in his/her credentials in order to gain access to the instance.

To allow a new user to sign up, simply set the **Allow users to sign up online** property to **true**. Signed up users will be automatically added to the default **sonar-users** group. You can specify another group by filling in the **Default user group** property.

Finally, you have to take the visibility of the source code into consideration. To prevent source code from getting displayed, set the **Import sources** property to **false**. You can later assign the special **Code viewers** role to allow specific groups or users to browse and view source code.

Creating users and groups

Log in as Administrator and click on the **Users** link, located under **SECURITY**, to get an overview of existing users. From here you can edit, delete, or add a new user. **Group management** can be found under **SECURITY:Groups**.

Browse to the **Groups management** screen and create a new group named **packt-group**. Users belonging to this group will be granted access to the code presented in this book. Next, create a user packt with password packt. Now, the user list will be repopulated, including the new user:

Users				
Login	Name	Email	Groups	Operations
admin	Administrator		sonar-administrators, sonar-users (select)	edit | change password | delete
packt	packt		packt-group, sonar-users (select)	edit | change password | delete

From the **Groups** column, click on **select** to add **packt-group** to the user's groups and save.

Managing project roles

Sonar manages security at four standard levels as shown under **Configuration | SECURITY**:

- **Users**
- **Groups**
- **Global Roles**
- **Project Roles**

Global Roles include one default **Administrator** role that grants a user every administrative right that has to do with the configuration and personalization of the instance. As a global administrator, you may configure every aspect of the instance, but you may not access some projects depending on their configuration.

Sonar features three default Project Roles—**Administrators**, **Users**, and **Code viewers**. Every project in Sonar is attached with a set of these three roles and different user groups can be assigned to each one. For example, if there are two teams, A and B, working on separate projects, you could create two groups, group-a and group-b, and assign them to roles on their corresponding projects.

Default roles for new projects

Role	Users	Groups
Administrators Ability to perform administration functions for a project by accessing its settings.	(select)	sonar-administrators (select)
Users Ability to navigate through every service of a project, except viewing source code and settings.	(select)	Anyone, sonar-users (select)
Code viewers Ability to view source code of a project.	(select)	Anyone, sonar-users (select)

Projects

Project	Role: Administrators	Role: Users	Role: Code viewers
No data			

by SonarSource ⟐ - Open Source LGPL ⟐ - v.2.11 - Plugins ⟐ - Documentation ⟐ - Ask a question ⟐

Backing up your data

It is crucial for the administrator to prepare a back up and restore plan in case of data loss or corruption. Sonar offers a backup and restore solution for its configuration data, but filesystem and database backups have to be taken care of manually, by the system's administrator.

Sonar instance configuration backup

Log in to Sonar as administrator, click on the **Configuration** link on the top of the dashboard, and then click on **Backup** from the left-hand side menu under the **SYSTEM** options. Click on the **Backup** button to download the instance's configuration in XML format. Restore the downloaded XML file in another Sonar instance to duplicate the configuration of a previous install.

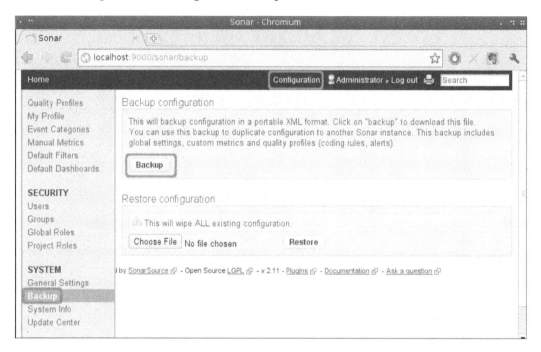

Filesystem backup

At filesystem level, keep a backup of the $SONAR_HOME directory at frequent intervals. This can be automated via cron jobs on Linux or by using Windows Backup on Windows.

For more sophisticated backup solutions, have a look at Wikipedia's comprehensive list of backup software at http://en.wikipedia.org/wiki/List_of_backup_software, either free or proprietary, for various operating systems.

Backing up the MySQL sonar database

Backup and restore on MySQL is done with the `mysqldump` and `mysqlimport` command-line tools respectively:

- `mysqldump`:

  ```
  $ mysqldump -u [username] -p [password] [dbname] > [backup.sql]
  ```

- `mysqlimport`:

  ```
  $ mysqlimport -u [username] -p [password] [dbname] backup.sql
  ```

To create the `sonar` database, open a terminal or get a command prompt if you are on Windows, and enter the following command:

```
$ mysqldump -u sonar -p sonar > sonar-backup.sql
```

To restore an existing `sonar` database, import the `sonar-backup.sql` file by entering the following command:

```
$ mysqlimport -u sonar -p sonar sonar-backup.sql
```

To rebuild the database from scratch type:

```
$ mysql -u sonar -p sonar < sonar-backup.sql
```

When executing the preceding commands, enter your MySQL's administrator password when prompted. Exercise caution, especially with the `import` command, as it can overwrite existing schemas.

Extending Sonar with plugins

Sonar features a very streamlined plugin installation process from within the platform's web update center—although a server restart is still mandatory. Next, we will install the Useless Code Tracker plugin by Olivier Gaudin. In short, this plugin calculates and reports on total duplicated lines inside a Java project. After installation, a new Useless Code widget will be available for customizing the Sonar dashboard.

To manage plugins, log in to Sonar as administrator and click on the **Update Center** link under the **SYSTEM** section. The **Update Center** section provides plugins and system information separated on the following four tabs:

- **Installed Plugins**: List of currently installed plugins
- **Available Plugins**: All available plugins in the Sonar library

- **Plugin Updates**: List of plugins that need updating
- **System Updates**: Information on new platform updates

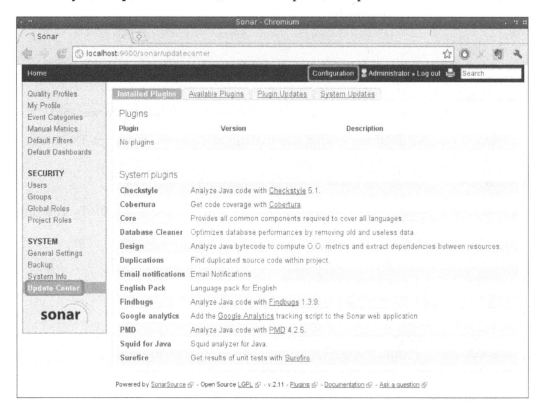

Installing the Useless Code Tracker plugin

From the **Update Center** section, click on the **Available Plugins** tab and scroll down to find the **Useless Code Tracker** plugin under the **Additional Metrics** category. Click on the plugin's name to expand a nested panel containing detailed information about the plugin such as **Author**, **License**, **Links**, and **Version**:

Useless Code Tracker	Find duplicated source code within project.
License:	GNU LGPL 3
Author:	SonarSource
Links:	Homepage Issue Tracker
Version:	0.4 (Aug 6, 2011)
Install	

Click on the **Install** button to initiate the installation process. When the installation has been completed, you will be prompted to restart the Sonar server in order to pick up the new plugin. In Windows, simply restart the service from Windows services. In Linux, stop the server by entering the following command:

```
$SONAR_HOME/bin/linux-x86-32/sonar.sh stop
```

Wait for the server to stop:

```
Stopping sonar...
Waiting for sonar to exit...
Stopped sonar.
```

Then start it again:

```
$SONAR_HOME/bin/linux-x86-32/sonar.sh start
```

To verify if the plugin is installed correctly, log in again and browse to the **Installed Plugins** screen from the **Update Center** section:

Installed Plugins	Available Plugins	Plugin Updates	System Updates

Plugins

Plugin	Version	Description
Useless Code Tracker	0.4	Find duplicated source code within project.

If everything works as expected, you will notice a new entry under **Plugins** featuring the newly installed plugin. To uninstall a plugin, simply click on its name to expand a details panel and then click on the **Uninstall** button. Uninstallation and plugin updates both require a restart of the Sonar server.

Upgrading Sonar from the Update Center section

To check if a new version of the platform has been released, visit the **Update Center** section and select the **System Updates** tab. If there is a new version available, an information panel with release information and installation details appears similar to the one depicted in the following screenshot:

Installed Plugins	Available Plugins	Plugin Updates	System Updates

Sonar 2.11

Date:	Oct 3, 2011
Release Notes ⌐ :	Sonar CPD to check cross project duplications, TimeMachine 2.0, suppress analysis snapshots, Sonar Server ID
How to upgrade:	Download ⌐ and install Sonar 2.11 after having carefully read the upgrade guide.

Updated on Wed Oct 26 11:23:33 EEST 2011. Refresh

Checking compatibility of plugins

It is possible for some plugins to require an update before upgrading to the new Sonar version or to be rendered obsolete and uninstalled. The **How to upgrade** section under the **System Updates** tab lists these plugins which should all be updated or uninstalled before proceeding with the platform's upgrade. After updating/uninstalling said plugins, stop the Sonar server or the Sonar service, if you are in Windows:

```
$ SONAR_HOME/bin/linux-x86-32/sonar.sh stop
```

Upgrading to latest Sonar version

Next, download the new Sonar version and unzip it in a new separate directory, let's say $NEW_SONAR_HOME.

 Before proceeding, make sure that the Sonar server is stopped and back up both the Sonar server and the MySQL database as described earlier in this chapter.

Copy the `sonar.properties` and `wrapper.conf` files from `$SONAR_HOME/conf` to `$NEW_SONAR_HOME/conf`.

Copy the `extensions/plugins` and `extensions/rules` directories from `$SONAR_HOME/conf` to `$NEW_SONAR_HOME/conf`.

If Sonar is deployed inside a J2EE Application Server, build the Sonar web application by executing the following script and deploy the generated `war` file to the application server:

```
$ NEW_SONAR_HOME/war/build-war
```

If you are in Windows, start the Sonar service from Windows services. In Linux, start the new server instance by using the following command:

```
$ NEW_SONAR_HOME/bin/linux-x86-32/sonar.sh start
```

Then, browse to `http://localhost:9000/setup` and follow the instructions.

 Completing the upgrade process

For the upgrade process to complete, it is necessary to perform an analysis on one of your projects.

Summary

In this chapter, we went through the installation process of the Sonar platform, configured a MySQL database to store Sonar data, and made a backup of our new instance. To meet the needs of an enterprise development environment, we further secured our instance, limited access to configuration and system settings, and created sample groups and users.

Finally, we focused on maintenance tasks such as installing plugins and updating the platform by using Sonar's **Update Center**.

In the next chapter, we will put our fresh instance to the test by analyzing projects with all available methods, customize the Sonar dashboard, and configure its widgets and interface components.

3
Analyzing your First Project

In this chapter, we will go through the process of analyzing a project, using all three methods that Sonar offers. We will take a closer look at the parameterization of each method and ways to run it. Having analyzed a project, it is time to get familiar with the dashboard. So next, we will browse to the dashboard, configure it to our liking, and manage all the available widgets that come with the default Sonar installation. Then, we will look at all the widgets and the insight they provide in greater detail.

Knowing how to set up an analysis and configure the dashboard, it is time to feed Sonar with some more projects to analyze. Having populated the dashboard with a handful of projects, a reorganization of the view is in order.

Finally, we will eliminate some common violations and apply a version change to one of our projects by triggering a Sonar event during the next analysis. The Sonar Time Machine component tracks and shows these events along with other information about the project's lifetime.

In this chapter we will cover:

- Installing and using a Java runner
- Installing and analyzing a project with Maven
- Project analysis with Ant
- Browsing the Sonar web interface
- Sonar components — an overview
- Anatomy of the dashboard
- Eliminating your first violations

The `commons-lang` Apache library will serve as the first test project to be imported into the Sonar platform. So, before we start, head to `http://commons.apache.org/lang/download_lang.cgi`, download the `commons-lang3-3.0.1-src.zip` ZIP file, and extract it.

Alternatively, if you are using a source code repository system such as Subversion, you can check out the source code with the following svn command:

```
svn checkout http://svn.apache.org/repos/asf/commons/proper/lang/trunk
commons-lang3
```

If the repository has been relocated, browse to http://commons.apache.org/lang/ source-repository.html.

Using a Java runner

Project analysis via java-runner is ideal for quick one-offs, especially for projects that are not under constant development, and continuous inspection of quality is not a requirement. A scenario would be to fire the procedure once, assess the results, and then decide whether the project will be put under deeper monitoring followed by a new development cycle.

While this method is ideal for quick one-off code auditions, it is not recommended in the long run, because it does not take any unit tests into account and does not integrate well in team environments. Consider java-runner as a supplement and not the core method of the platform.

Configuring the runner

First download the Sonar java-runner plugin from http://repository. codehaus.org/org/codehaus/sonar-plugins/sonar-runner/1.1/ sonar-runner-1.1.zip and unzip it. Do not unzip it within Sonar's plugins directory, because it will be detected as a plugin by the server, and the server will throw an exception. We will refer back to the plugin's installation directory with the $SONAR_RUNNER_HOME system variable.

Next open the $SONAR_RUNNER_HOME/conf/sonar-runner.properties file and edit the Default Sonar Server and MySQL sections as follows:

```
#----- Default Sonar server
sonar.host.url=http://SERVER_IP_ADDRESS:9000/sonar
...
#----- MySQL
sonar.jdbc.url=jdbc:mysql://SERVER_IP_ADDRESS:3306/sonar?useUnicode=tr
ue&amp;characterEncoding=utf8
sonar.jdbc.driver=com.mysql.jdbc.Driver
....
#----- Global database settings
sonar.jdbc.username=sonar
sonar.jdbc.password=sonar
```

Now the runner is configured. To verify this, execute the `java-runner` command with the `-h` switch to display basic usage information—the command is the same for Windows:

```
$ $SONAR_RUNNER_HOME/bin/sonar-runner -h
usage: sonar-runner [options]
Options:
 -h,--help              Display help information
 -X,--debug             Produce execution debug output
 -D,--define <arg>      Define property
```

Setting up a Sonar server for remote connections

Before moving on, it is vital to ensure that if the client machine from which the runner will execute, can connect to the remote Sonar server and the hosted MySQL instance. This has to be ensured in order to post analysis results back to the Sonar server and persist them in the configured database.

 If you are using Windows, whenever you are instructed to open a command prompt or a terminal to execute a command, run the `cmd` command to open a Windows terminal and continue from there.

Open a command prompt and type the `telnet` command:

```
$ telnet IP_ADDRESS PORT
```

`IP_ADDRESS` is the Sonar's server IP and `PORT` is the port on which the server listens, defaulted to 9000. If the telnet connection fails, ensure that the Sonar server is up and running, and that no firewall is blocking incoming connections at port 9000.

To test MySQL connectivity, enter the following command, filling in `sonar` as the password when prompted:

```
$ mysql IP_ADDRESS -u sonar -p
```

If MySql is installed on the same machine, you can alternatively enter the following command:

```
$ mysql -h localhost -u sonar -p
```

If a connection is established, the `mysql>` command prompt should appear ready to accept user input. We are now ready to configure and start `java-runner` from the client machine. If the connection is refused, read on on how to set up MySQL properly in order to accept remote connections.

First, you have to locate the `my.cnf` MySQL configuration file, which resides inside MySQL's installation directory. On Linux systems, this file is usually under the `/etc/mysq/` directory. In Windows, the file is located under `C:\Program Files\ MySQL` — the default installation directory.

Open the file with the command, or use the editor of your choice to edit the file:

```
$ sudo nano /etc/mysql/my.cnf
```

Then, with *Ctrl* + *W*, search for the `bind` keyword until you locate the following line:

```
    bind-address            =IP_ADDRESS
```

Replace the preceding line with a commented one like:

```
    # bind-address          =IP_ADDRESS
```

Next, connect to MySQL and grant privileges to the client machine from where the `java-runner` will run:

```
$ mysql -u sonar -p
mysql> GRANT ALL on sonar.* TO sonar@'CLIENT_IP_ADDRESS'    IDENTIFIED BY 'sonar';
```

Finally, edit the `/etc/hosts` file and add the client's IP address and hostname as follows:

```
    CLIENT_IP_ADDRESS               CLIENT_HOSTNAME
```

Configuring the project

So far we have configured the `java-runner`, and the Sonar server is now ready to accept incoming projects. The final step of the process is to create a configuration file for the `commons-lang` project. Notice that every project up for analysis requires its own configuration file located under its base directory and specifically named after `sonar-project.`properties.

The following snippet is a version of the file broken up into four sections and edited for the `commons-lang` project. The `$COMMONS_LANG` variable is the project's base directory and you will have to substitute it with a real filesystem location:

```
# Section 1: required metadata
sonar.projectKey=commons lang
sonar.projectName=Commons Lang 3
sonar.projectVersion=3.0

# Section 2: project directories
# path to source directories (required)
sources=$COMMONS_LANG/src/main/java

# path to test source directories (optional)
tests=$COMMONS_LANG/src/test/java

# path to project binaries (optional), for example directory of Java
# bytecode
binaries=$COMMONS_LANG/target/classes

# Section 3: Java and libraries settings
# optional comma-separated list of paths to libraries. Only path to
JAR file
# and path to directory of classes are supported.
#libraries=path/to/library.jar

# Uncomment those lines if some features of java 5 or java 6 like
# annotations, enum, ...
# are used in the source code to be analysed
sonar.java.source=1.5
sonar.java.target=1.5

# Section 4: Advanced parameters
# Uncomment this line to analyse a project which is not a java
project.
# The value of the property must be the key of the language.
#sonar.language=cobol

# Advanced parameters
#my.property=value
```

It's mandatory to use forward slashes (/), even in Windows, wherever you enter path names in configuration files. For example, path `C:\dev` would become `C:/dev`.

The preceding snippet has been broken into the following sections:

- `Section 1: required metadata`: This section provides basic information about the project. These values show up on the dashboard. Changing the version number and rerunning the analysis triggers an event, which is shown on the dashboard and the Time Machine.

- `Section 2: project directories`: Fill in paths for source, test, and classes directories in this section. You can enter multiple source paths separated by commas. Although the test path is valid, the runner never runs them.

- `Section 3: Java and libraries settings`: In this section, enter paths to the library dependencies, if any. The Java 1.5 properties are uncommented because `commons-lang` uses Java 1.5 features.

- `Section 4: Advanced parameters`: For non-Java projects, uncomment and set the `sonar.language` property. Some valid settings would be `php`, `js`, and even `cobol`.

Moreover, with the `sonar.profile` property, you can overload the default server's setting and specify another profile for the project at hand. Use the `sonar.exclusions` property to exclude files in a comma-separated list from analysis — it supports wildcards and patterns. Finally, if security is an issue, set the `sonar.importIssues` to `false` to prevent project source code from being saved and displayed on the dashboard. The analysis results remain unaffected.

To run the analysis, save the `sonar-project.properties` file under the `$COMMONS_LANG` directory, open a command prompt, and execute the `sonar-runner` within the `$COMMONS_LANG` base directory:

```
commons-lang3$ /~/development/tools/sonar-runner-1.1/bin/sonar-runner
```

Sonar will immediately start scanning and analyzing code:

```
[INFO]   Database dialect class org.sonar.jpa.dialect.MySql
[INFO]   Initializing Hibernate
[INFO]   -------------  Analyzing Commons Lang 3
[INFO]   Selected quality profile : [name=Sonar way,language=java]
[INFO]   Configure maven plugins...
[INFO]   Compare to previous analysis
[INFO]   Compare over 5 days (2011-11-09)
```

```
[INFO]   Compare over 30 days (2011-10-15)
[INFO]   Sensor JavaSourceImporter...
[INFO]   Sensor JavaSourceImporter done: 32279 ms
...
[INFO]   Sensor TrackerSensor done: 1889 ms
[INFO]   Execute decorators...
[INFO]   ANALYSIS SUCCESSFUL, you can browse http://IP_ADDRESS:9000/
sonar
```

Analysis with the Sonar Maven plugin

Maven is a build system tool allowing developers and teams to build their projects in a uniform way. It is based on a common Project Object Model standardizing the structure of Java projects. Build settings, plugins, and library dependencies, all stored in a single pom.xml configuration file — the core of the Maven build system.

The mechanism of the Maven build system follows the notion of goals. For example, if you want to compile a project, you run Maven's mvn command with the compile goal as a parameter. Similarly, the mvn test command will compile and execute the project's unit tests, while mvn package builds go through the whole process from compiling and executing unit tests to packaging your final application. Its elegant build model enables extensions and plugins for every need and purpose. The Sonar Maven plugin adds the sonar goal, which triggers project analysis.

Installing Maven

Maven is available at http://maven.apache.org/download.html. Download any 3.x version (Maven 2 is still compatible with Sonar if you have it already installed), and extract it in the directory to which you wish to install Maven.

On Linux, add the MAVEN_HOME environment variable by adding the following lines to your .bashrc or .bash_profile. For example:

```
# maven MAVEN_HOME path
MAVEN_HOME=/usr/lib/apache-maven/apache-maven-3.0.3
PATH=$PATH:$MAVEN_HOME/bin
export PATH
# optional maven settings
# MAVEN_OPTS="-Xms256m -Xmx512m"
```

To reload the configuration, open a terminal and enter:

```
$ source ~/.bashrc
```

or

```
$ source ~/.bash_profile
```

respectively.

Finally, run:

```
$ mvn --version
```

to verify that Maven was installed successfully.

```
Apache Maven 3.0.3 (r1075438; 2011-02-28 19:31:09+0200)
Maven home: /usr/lib/apache-maven/apache-maven-3.0.3
```

To install Maven on Windows, follow the same steps by adding the MAVEN_HOME environment variable:

```
C:\Program Files\Apache Software Foundation\apache-maven-3.0.3
```

Some of the more important Maven commands are :

- mvn compile: Compiles java classes
- mvn test: Runs unit tests
- mvn package : Builds the project and creates a JAR file

Simply navigate to a Maven project's directory and run these commands from there.

Configuring the Sonar Maven plugin

The Sonar Maven plugin adds the following two new goals:

- sonar:help: Displays helpful information
- sonar:sonar: Performs project analysis

To activate the plugin, you will have to edit the settings.xml Maven configuration file located at $MAVEN_HOME/conf/settings.xml. Locate the <profiles> section and a new profile entry for the sonar goal as shown in the following snippet:

```
<profiles>
...
    <profile>
        <id>sonar</id>
```

```
<activation>
    <activeByDefault>true</activeByDefault>
</activation>
<properties>

    <!-- MySQL Settings  -->
        <sonar.jdbc.url>
            jdbc:mysql://localhost:3306/sonar?useUnicode=true&
            amp;characterEncoding=utf8
        </sonar.jdbc.url>
        <sonar.jdbc.driverClassName>com.mysql.jdbc.Driver</
        sonar.jdbc.driverClassName>
        <sonar.jdbc.username>sonar</sonar.jdbc.username>
        <sonar.jdbc.password>sonar</sonar.jdbc.password>

    <!-- Sonar server URL -->
    <sonar.host.url>
        http://localhost:9000
    </sonar.host.url>
</properties>
</profile>
...
</profiles>
```

The new profile is identified by its unique id element named sonar. The properties define MySQL connection settings and the URL of the Sonar server.

> **Memory size**
>
> If your machine runs out of memory, you can increase the Java heap memory size by using the MAVEN_OPTS environment variable as follows:
>
> MAVEN_OPTS="-Xmx512m -XX:MaxPermSize=128m"

The Sonar Maven goal is now activated and can be run by using the following command:

```
$ mvn sonar:sonar
```

Remember to navigate to the project's root directory, that is, where the pom.xml file resides for all Maven projects, before executing the command, and that the Sonar server is running.

If you wish to read more about the plugin, you can always visit the official website at `http://mojo.codehaus.org/sonar-maven-plugin/`.

Apart from Sonar, numerous Maven plugins offer different functionalities and useful additions for every taste and need, such as:

- `javadoc` generation in both HTML and PDF format
- Automatic class diagrams and call graphs
- Applying patch files to the source code

Performing the analysis

To perform a Sonar analysis for the `commons-lang` project, open a terminal, change directory to `$COMMONS_LANG`, and run `mvn sonar:sonar`. Here is some sample output from the console during the analysis to get a better idea of the process (the whole procedure should last for a couple of minutes):

```
[INFO] Scanning for projects...
[INFO]
[INFO] ------------------------------------------------------------
----------
[INFO] Building Commons Lang 3.1-SNAPSHOT
[INFO] ------------------------------------------------------------
----------
[INFO]
[INFO] --- sonar-maven-plugin:2.0:sonar (default-cli) @ commons-lang3
---
[INFO] Sonar version: 2.11
[INFO]   Database dialect class org.sonar.jpa.dialect.MySql
[INFO]   Initializing Hibernate
...
[INFO]   Sensor CoberturaSensor done: 2018 ms
[INFO]   Sensor Maven dependencies...
[INFO]   Sensor Maven dependencies done: 601 ms
[INFO]   Execute decorators...
[INFO]   ANALYSIS SUCCESSFUL, you can browse http://localhost:9000
...
[INFO] BUILD SUCCESS
...
```

Notice that Maven goes through the package goal first, executing tests and producing a new build, followed by sonar analysis.

After the analysis has been finished, the project is added to the web dashboard at `http://localhost:9000`.

Analysis with Ant

Apache Ant, `ant` in the command line, is one of the oldest Java build tools around. Chances are you might be using it already or have switched to a more modern system such as Maven or Gradle. To perform a Sonar analysis, you need to create a new Sonar Ant Task and define the configuration inside an `ant` script file. Then, add a new Ant target referencing the sonar configured task inside your project's build script and provide path information for source, binaries, and project libraries.

First, let's go through the installation process.

Installing Ant

In order to use Ant in conjunction with Sonar, the following requirements must be met:

- Ant 1.7.1 or higher
- Java 1.5 or higher
- Sonar 2.8 or higher

Download the latest Ant release from `http://ant.apache.org/bindownload.cgi` and uncompress it into a directory. On Linux, add the `ANT_HOME` environment variable to your PATH by editing `.bashrc` (or `.bash_profile`) accordingly. On Windows, add the variable by right-clicking on **My Computer | System Properties | Environment Variables**.

The section of the `.bashrc` file declaring the `ANT_HOME` variable is as follows:

```
# ANT_HOME environment variable
ANT_HOME=/usr/lib/ant/apache-ant-1.8.2
export ANT_HOME
PATH=$PATH:$ANT_HOME/bin
export PATH
```

Finally, reload the `.bashrc` configuration and run `ant -version` to verify the installation:

```
$ source ~/.bashrc
$ ant -version
```

Configuring and running Sonar analysis task

Download the Sonar Ant Task, `sonar-ant-task-1.2.jar`, from `http://docs.codehaus.org/display/SONAR/Analyse+with+Ant+Task` and put in your `$ANT_HOME/lib` directory.

Ant's build files are essentially XML files. We are not going to go into the details right now, all you need to know is that in Ant, we define tasks and targets pointing back to these tasks. Task definitions contain all necessary configurations required for a task to execute while the target parameterizes the task to meet each project's needs.

For Sonar, we must first define a task with server and database connection configuration. Every task is identified by a Uniform Resource Identifier—`antlib:org.sonar.ant` for the Sonar one. The target configuration section refers to the task by its URI and holds sources and binaries path configuration.

Modify the `build.xml` Ant script of your project and add the following section for Sonar (the highlighted lines should be modified to match your environment):

```
<project name="Your Project" >
...

    <!-- Define the Sonar task -->
    <taskdef uri="antlib:org.sonar.ant" resource="org/sonar/ant/
    antlib.xml">
        <classpath path="path/to/sonar/ant/task/lib" />
    </taskdef>

    <!-- Sonar MySQL connection -->
    <property name="sonar.jdbc.url" value="jdbc:mysql://localhost:
    3306/sonar?useUnicode=true&amp;characterEncoding=utf8" />
    <property name="sonar.jdbc.driverClassName" value="
    com.mysql.jdbc.Driver" />
    <property name="sonar.jdbc.username" value="sonar" />
    <property name="sonar.jdbc.password" value="sonar" />

    <!-- Sonar server URL -->
    <property name="sonar.host.url" value="http://localhost:9000" />

    <!-- Sonar target -->
    <target name="sonar">
```

```
<!-- the sources path is required -->
<property name="sonar.sources" value="list of source
directories separated by a comma" />

<!-- optional paths for compiled classes, tests, and
libraries -->
<property name="sonar.projectName" value="this value overrides
the name defined in Ant root node" />
<property name="sonar.binaries" value="compiled classses
directory" />
<property name="sonar.tests" value="unit tests" />
<property name="sonar.libraries" value="project library
dependencies separated by comma" />
...

<sonar:sonar key="org.example:example" version="0.1-SNAPSHOT"
xmlns:sonar="antlib:org.sonar.ant"/>

</target>
...
</project>
```

Notice that the `sonar.sources` property is mandatory. Before running the task, make sure to build the project once so as to generate compiled classes and unit tests results. Otherwise, they will be omitted from the Sonar analysis task.

To run the analysis, move to the project base directory and execute the following command:

```
$ ant sonar
```

Browsing the Sonar web interface

Now you can add your own project to Sonar, or download open source ones to demo the platform and play with the dashboard. Verify that the Sonar server is running, point your browser at `http://localhost:9000`, and log in to Sonar.

The Sonar home page represents all analyzed projects in a table list form. Click on any table column to sort the project list or click on the leftmost star icon to make a project favorite.

This project list is essentially the default view, or filtered, configured, and defaulted by Sonar. The following list gives a brief explanation of each column:

- **Name**: The name of the project is defined inside the `pom.xml` Maven file under the `<name/>` element.
- **Version**: This is the `<version/>` element from `pom.xml`.

- **Lines of code (LOC)**: This specifies the total lines of code excluding documentation.

- **Rules compliance**: This is a percentile aggregated value reflecting overall quality.

- **Build date**: This specifies the date on which the analysis took place. It displays only a time HH:MM value, if the project was analyzed today.

- **Links**: This specifies the Maven configurable project links pointing to sources, project home site, bug tracker, and so on.

Rules Compliance Index (RCI)

Sonar collects data from three different analysis engines, which evaluate different weighted code violations. Each rule is configurable and affects quality at different levels based on its configuration.

Sonar processes the collected data and finalizes the calculation by aggregating all results into one single metric, the Rules Compliance Index. The evaluation formula for the RCI is as follows:

$$RCI = 100 - \left(\frac{weighted\ violations}{lines\ of\ code} * 100 \right)$$

To point out changes through time, small arrows sit next to the columns to show whether a measure has decreased or increased since the last analysis.

Additionally, you can view changes over a given period of time by selecting the desired period from the top-right drop-down list. Differential values next to each measure will appear by showing how each measure has changed over the selected period of time:

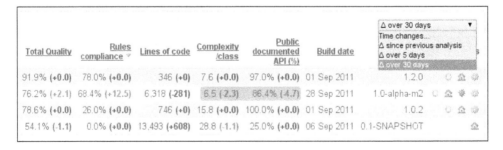

Each tab on top of the Sonar home page browses to a different filter. Sonar comes with three preconfigured filters:

- **Projects**: Tabular list of all analyzed projects
- **Treemap**: Color and size-sensitive treemap project view
- **Favorites**: Your favorite projects are stored here for quick access

We have already detailed the **Projects** filter with **Favorites** being an identical subset of the first. Next, we will examine the **Treemap** gadget.

The treemap gadget

To better grasp the usefulness of the treemap gadget, add a few more projects into your Sonar installation:

- **Enforcer**: `http://maven.apache.org/enforcer/source-repository.html`
- **Commons BeanUtils**: `http://commons.apache.org/beanutils/source-repository.html`
- **Commons Chain**: `http://commons.apache.org/chain/source-repository.html`
- **Commons Collections**: `http://commons.apache.org/collections/source-repository.html`

Download and extract each project's source, move into the base directory, and run the following two commands to build and perform sonar analysis:

```
$ mvn package
$ mvn sonar:sonar
```

When the goals have been completed, browse to the Sonar home page to view the new analyzed projects and click on the second **Treemap** tab.

The **treemap** displays information at project level, drilling down to package and class level. The size and color of the boxes are project-sensitive measures and qualities. Simply select a measure from the corresponding drop-down lists and watch the treemap adapting to the new values. In the following map, the size of the boxes is proportional to the total lines of code while the color's green hue is proportional to test coverage.

Large boxes mean more lines of code, while greener boxes interpret to a higher test coverage percentage.

The color levels range in the following scale from worst to best:

Red > Yellow > Green

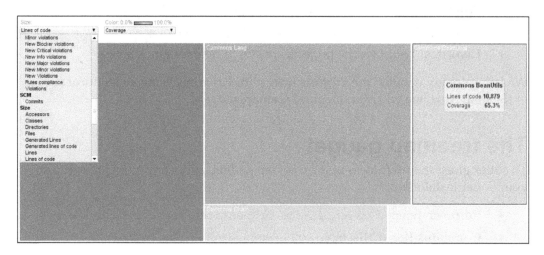

The treemap gadget is not a static component; on the contrary, its generic design allows visualization of different resources. As a matter of fact, you can treemap at project, package, and even at class level.

Filtering your projects

To manage filters, you have to log in to Sonar as an administrator. Now, on the top-right section, the filters management hotbar becomes available. Next, create a new filter including only the Apache Commons projects, leaving out Enforcer and any other projects that you own.

Select **Add filter** to navigate to the filter configuration settings screen:

Fill in the **Name** field with the value Apache Commons. This will be the name of the filter and the tab's title. Check the **Shared** checkbox, if you wish to make it available to everyone, or leave it unchecked to keep it private.

Next, in the **Search for** section, verify that the **Projects** checkbox is checked and click on the **Advanced Search** link at the bottom to open up additional filtering settings. From here, you can filter resources such as projects, packages, classes, and static files by name.

To include only the **Apache Commons** libraries, fill in the **Resource key like** input field with the value `*commons-*` and click on **Save & Preview** (it supports the * wildcard):

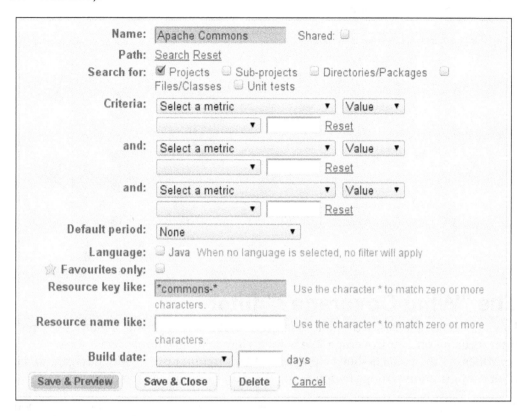

Now, at the bottom of the **Display** panel, only the four Apache Commons projects appear. From here, you can select how the projects will be rendered, either as a **Table** or with the **Treemap** component. Add new metric columns and select the **Default sorted column**. When you are happy with the settings, click on **Save & Close** to save the filter. Then notice how it is added next to the **Favorites** tab.

Use the column controls to rearrange columns or remove them from the list. In the example screen, the **Build Date** column was removed, and the **Public documented API (%)** column was added with its order altered and bringing it forward immediately after **Lines of code**.

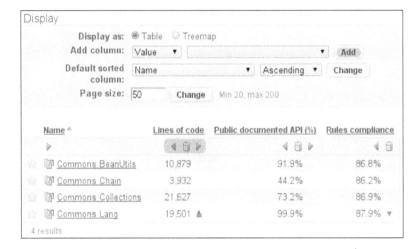

The "What Coverage?" filter

Having learned the basics of filter management, it is time to create a metrics-oriented filter focusing on Test Coverage. We want a view with all complex class files regardless of the projects they belong to and lack in unit tests. Again, navigate to the filter configuration settings by following the **Add filter** link on the right.

Name the filter as What Coverage? and check only the **Files/Classes** checkbox. Then, add two criteria rows. For the first one select **Coverage** from the drop-down list with a **Value Less than 25.0**—for the Coverage metric the 25 value is treated as a percentage. For the second one select **Complexity** with a **Value Greater than 100.0**—we are looking for really complex classes here. Finally, click on **Save & Preview** to move on to the **Display** settings.

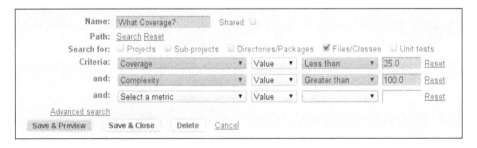

For this kind of filter, visual feedback is appropriate. Select the **Treemap** radio button to have the classes rendered by the treemap gadget. We want complex and untested classes appearing as large and red boxes. To achieve this effect, select **Complexity** from the drop-down list for **Size** and **Coverage** for **Color**. Click on **Change** to view the final result and **Save & Close** to save the filter:

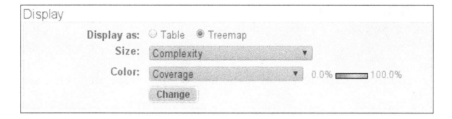

Each box inside the treemap represents a complex and untested class. Mouse over the boxes to get the exact complexity and coverage values. To drill down to the source code, click on any box and a new window pops up presenting the file's source code. The regions where test coverage is lacking, are highlighted.

As you can see, large red boxes are fairly complex classes with minimum test coverage and they require attention.

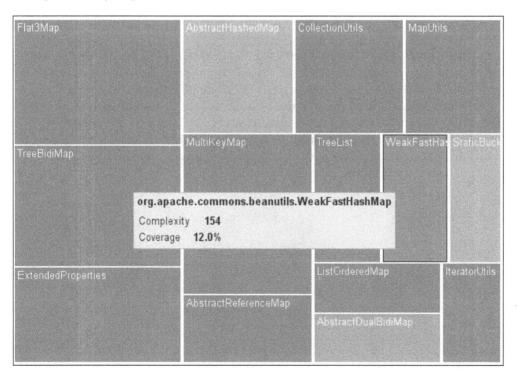

Sonar components— an overview

Clicking on a project's name from the home page gets you to the project's dashboard. The default configuration consists of a two-column layout with the basic widgets. The menu on the left is split into two sections—project navigation and configuration. Configuration settings and dashboard/widgets management are available to project administrators only. Before we go into dashboard details, let's have a quick look at the available components starting with the top left:

- **Dashboard**: Every project's entry point
- **Components**: Drill down one level, for example, from project to package level
- **Violations Drilldown**: Violations indexer
- **Time Machine**
- **Clouds**
- **Design**
- **Hotspots**
- **Libraries**

Dashboard

This is the default view when you browse into a project. It is a portlet-like setup hosting numerous Sonar widgets. It is fully configurable and enables you to create customized dashboards suited to your needs. For instance, you can change the layout from a single column up to a three-columns layout; rearrange, add, or remove widgets limiting information or extending it; and of course, you can preserve these changes to a new custom dashboard leaving the default as it is. Every new dashboard you create or share with other users will appear immediately under the default one on the left menu:

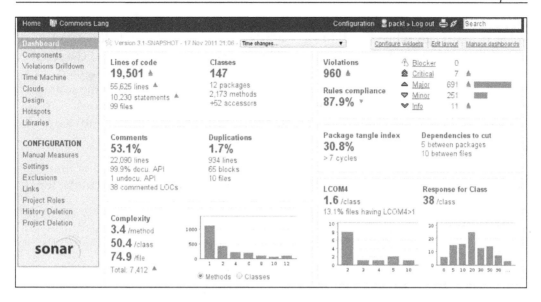

Components

The components view drills down one level to project level. For example, when viewing a Java project's dashboard by clicking on a component, Sonar drills down to package level. The project along with some accumulated metrics appears on the top of the components view. Then, below the project, a data table breaks down all project packages. Turning **Customize ON** at the top left allows editing of the columns of the data table. Besides the data table, the packages are also visualized via the treemap gadget. Click on the treemap to drill down further to a class-level dashboard.

Violations drilldown

The **Violations Drilldown** component acts as an indexer, displaying all project violations sorted from different perspectives. The component features four different sections — two at the top and two at the bottom. The top left-panel provides an overview of violation totals by **Severity** from **Blocked** down to the less significant **Info**. On the top-right, the actual violations appear ordered again by **Severity**. The counter next to each violation represents how many times it was encountered in the source code. Clicking on **Severity** or a specific violation causes the component to filter and refresh the presented data. For example, if you click on **Major,** only major violations and their totals will appear. The filter also applies to the bottom section showing only packages and classes with **Major** violations.

The bottom section is self-explanatory. On the left, there are packages and violation totals per package, while the right section lists classes sorted by violation count. Select any package and the right panel will refresh to present its violated classes. Select a class and the source code viewer component will render a highlighted version of the file's source right below. Try it and see for yourself, how the source viewer is clever enough to precisely highlight the lines that have violations. Moreover, along with the highlight at line level, Sonar offers additional advice on what caused the violation and some common methods on how to fix it.

Finally, you can adjust the view to represent violation for a given period of time by selecting the appropriate period from the **Time changes** drop-down list at the top:

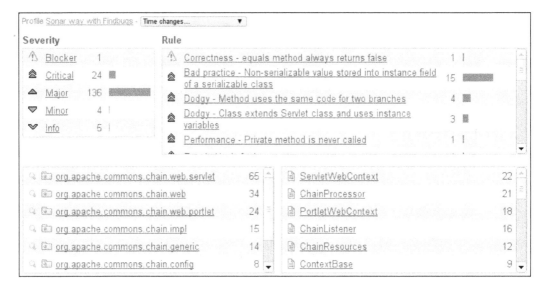

Time Machine

The Sonar **Time Machine** is one of the most valuable and interesting components in the Sonar family.

Data metrics are useful, but they are isolated from a project's lifetime as they hold little information in the long run. What matters the most is the evolution of code and how the seven axes of quality are affected during the development period in accordance to team size, implemented features, project requirements, and working man hours.

As `SonarSource.com` puts it, "replaying the past" is an essential key feature, which enables the manager to observe development progress in time, and drive resources with increased efficiency. For example, suppose evaluation of a Sonar analysis of your new project reveals a fair amount of uncovered and untested complex code. This on its own does not say much. Was it always this way? Is this how this development team approaches projects? Or something else has happened? Examining the history on the Time Machine reveals that in the past code coverage was always increasing proportionally to complexity. There were some minor gaps here and there, but basically at all milestones coverage was above a healthy 75 percent. So, the team used to respect and treat complexity with care. A thorough investigation reveals that team composition has changed and the *i-write-tests* developer has been moved to the Q&A department.

> *Metrics are created from code, but the code is written by people. The Time Machine connects numbers and measures to real life development matters such as project requirements, team composition, development trends, and management. Indeed, it is a worthy manager's assistant.*

The following screenshot depicts the **Time Machine** component in detail. By default, the component focuses on historical data about **Complexity**, **Coverage**, and **Rules compliance**. But you are not restricted only to these. Below the component sits the measurements list from which you can select the metrics you need. All measures are indexed by topics such as **Documentation**, **Rules**, and **Duplication** among others. Click on the **Compare on chart** button at the bottom of the page to refresh the Time Machine and display the evolution of your selected metrics. If you are logged in as an administrator, click on the **Set as default** link to save your preferences as defaults for the component.

Major project events such as version and quality profile changes are displayed on top of the chart. You can hide or select specific events from the drop-down list. Alternatively, click through the calendar to select specific dates. Only dates on which an analysis was performed will be active though.

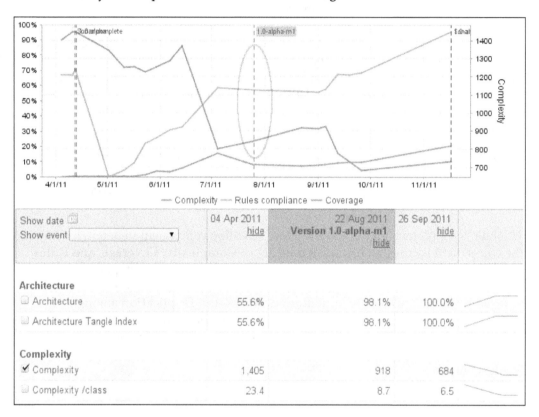

Clouds

Clouds is an extremely informational component that allows identifying dangerous classes at a glance. It represents classes as a tag-cloud with tag size and color depending on the selected measure—**Coverage** or **Rules compliance**—and the selected aspect—**Quick wins** or **Top risk**. Make your selections from the drop-down list and the radio buttons, and the Cloud will re-render instantly.

These are the options that you can select from the **Color** section:

- **Coverage**: Color is more red when Coverage is lacking
- **Rules Compliance**: Color is more red when violations increase

The following are the radio buttons available:

- **Quick wins**: Tag font size is proportional to lines of code
- **Top Risk**: Tag font size is proportional to complexity

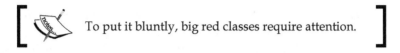 To put it bluntly, big red classes require attention.

Click on any class to view its source code inside the Sonar source viewer. The code is highlighted accordingly, based on the selected measure:

Design

Usually, warnings in the design department tend to be the most serious and difficult to resolve. One of them is the dependency cycle. A dependency cycle occurs when Class A constructs or calls a method of Class B and vice versa. It is a basic hierarchy problem, which if left unmanaged ends up with non-modularized code that cannot be re-used. Lack of cohesion and unneeded coupling is a tight knot to solve, especially if it reaches Gordian levels. Refer to the component often, and cut dependencies early before they accumulate.

Horizontal rows represent modules, packages, or files. Select a row to highlight the matrix according to incoming and outgoing dependencies. The matrix values count file dependencies among packages. The dependency path is color-coded:

Green > uses Blue > uses Yellow

The sample project, as shown in the following screenshot, has some issues since the `*.jaipur.core` package depends on the `*.jaipur.impl` package and vice versa. Cycling dependencies are identified by the red highlighted values inside the matrix.

Select the highlighted dependency numbers to view the dependency relationships of the java classes at the bottom of the component.

Hotspots

The **Hotspots** component collects and sorts violation totals and measures. Essentially, it is a collection of the top five listed widgets with each widget focusing on a different axis of quality. The **Hotspots** lists help illuminate where to start fixing things cost-wise. Use it to answer the following questions:

- Which is the class with the most violations?
- Which class contains the most duplicated code?
- Which class lacks coverage or has the highest complexity?

Libraries

The **Libraries** component simply lists project's library dependencies. You can use the filter at the top of the page to search for a specific library or click on the **Usages** link to view projects that use the selected library.

Anatomy of the dashboard

The Sonar dashboard is the entry point for every project. The default two-column layout hosts numerous widgets that describe quality and give you insight on different metrics. The top two widgets provide statistics on code size and violation totals by severity.

As shown in the following screenshot, the `commons-lang` project takes up **19,499** lines of code across **99** files. There are **147** classes in total featuring **2.173** methods via **52** accessors.

> **Accessors methods**
>
> Accessors are all getter methods that follow the standard JavaBean pattern. Such methods expose private objects' properties. For example, the `public String getMessage();` method is an accessor to the the private string message property.
>
> The higher the accessor count, the more open an API is.

Selecting a severity from the violations summary on the right, browse to the violations drill-down component already filtered by the selected level.

Lines of code	Classes	Violations	Blocker	0
19,499	**147**	**943** ⚑	Critical	9
55,624 lines	12 packages		Major	689
10,229 statements	2,173 methods	**Rules compliance**	Minor	242
99 files	+52 accessors	**87.9%** ▾	Info	3

The next group of widgets displays general information about **Documentation**, **Design**, and **Complexity**. Select any measurement in the **Comments** or **Duplications** sections to open the resource viewer and identify the undocumented and duplicated lines of code. The dependencies widget is an overview of dependencies and package cycling. Click on a measurement to navigate to the **Design** component.

On the second row on the left, the **Complexity** widget breaks down the complexity at package, class, and method level. Click on a value to drill down to classes ordered in a descending order by complexity—method or class total. Also, watch the distribution chart for any suspicious spikes. A healthy distribution for methods would be to have a few complex methods and many simpler ones, while for classes a linear to average distribution seems more normal.

Through the book, we will thoroughly discuss and utilize the object-oriented LCOM4 and **Response for class (RFC)** metrics, which govern architecture and design. LCOM4 is one of the four variations in the **Lack of cohesion methods (LCOM)** family.

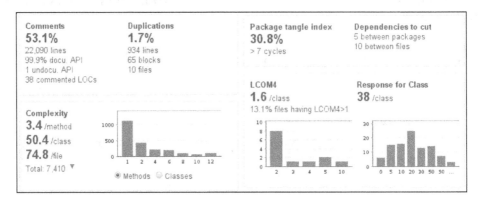

The code coverage widget displays unit test statistics over successes, failures, and duration. Click on the coverage links to inspect classes that lack testing. Then, select any class to have the resource viewer highlight untested lines and branches.

The event widget highlights events during the lifetime of the project. Version and quality profile changes are automatically registered by Sonar, but you can also add manual project events by clicking on the **Add an event** link at the bottom of the widget. Fill in the form with the event's details by giving it a name and description, and click on **Create** to save it.

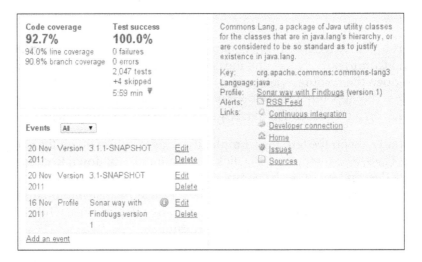

Layout and widget arrangement

Log in as an administrator and browse any project dashboard. Click on the **Manage Dashboards** link located at the top of the page to manage your dashboards. A list with all your custom dashboards will appear allowing you to edit them, delete, or configure widgets.

To create a new dashboard, fill in the **Name** and **Description** (optional) fields inside the form at the right of the page and click on the **Create Dashboard** link. If you want to share the dashboard with other sonar users, do not forget to check the shared checkbox. Your dashboard will be created and Sonar will prompt you to select the widgets you want it to host from a comprehensive list. You can filter the list by clicking one of the top **None**, **Design**, **History**, **Rules**, or **Tests** links. Read the available widget description and click on the **Add widget** link to add it to the dashboard:

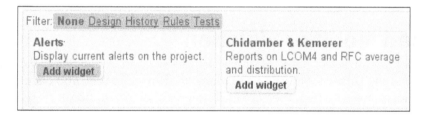

Some widgets allow further parameterization by clicking on the **Edit** link on top of them. For example, if you select the **Timeline** widget, you can edit which three metrics will be displayed. Another useful and fully customizable widget is the **Custom Measures** widget. Add it and select which metrics you want it to display. Notice that a widget can be added many times. It is possible to add two **Timeline** widgets tracking historical data on different aspects, for instance having two timelines tracking metrics on **Complexity** and **Unit Testing**. Finally, click-and-drag around any widget by its header to reposition it either vertically or horizontally on a different column. When you are done, click on the **Back** button to navigate to the dashboard link.

For complex projects, you could create separate dashboards entirely focused on a single aspect featuring the **Overview** dashboard, **Coverage** dashboard, and so on.

To reconfigure the widgets, click on the **Configure widgets** link at the top. To change the dashboard's layout, click on the **Edit layout** link and select one from the available five. Avoid the single column one because in most cases it produces dashboards that require excessive scrolling in order to view all widgets.

Eliminating your first violations

Now we will pick the commons-lang project that we imported into Sonar earlier and eliminate a few violations. Then, we'll run a new analysis and get visual feedback afterwards through the web interface. Of course, you are free to choose any project and try to eliminate similar violations. Before we start the process of editing source files, here is what the **Violations** widget reads:

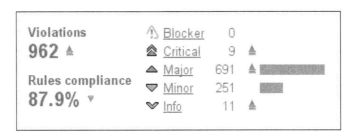

Unused modifier violation

From the left menu, select the **Violations Drilldown** component. Select the **Info** severity, find the **Unused Modifier** violations on the right panel, and click them to see the exact classes at which they are encountered. Sonar will find Builder.java inside the package org.apache.commons.lang3.builder and ExceptionContext. java in the package org.apache.commons.lang3.exception. Click on the filenames to open up the source viewer and drill down to the exact line where each violation is encountered.

Open the Builder.java file and delete the public declaration at line 88, since it will be calculated by the java compiler:

```
88    public T build();
```

This line will become:

```
88    T build();
```

Do the same for the ExceptionContext.java interface and delete the public declaration at line 49:

```
49    public ExceptionContext addContextValue(String label, Object
50 value);
```

This line will become:

```
49    ExceptionContext addContextValue(String label, Object value);
```

Filter again by selecting the **Major** severity to review major violations. Among others Sonar finds:

- **Modified Order**: Major violation in `FormatCache.java` inside the `package org.apache.commons.lang3.time`

- **Correctness - Repeated conditional tests**: Major violation in `DurationFormatUtils,java` in the package `org.apache.commons.lang3.time`

Modified Order violation

The **Modified Order** violation means that a method or a variable declaration does not follow Java standards. For example, in `FormatCache.java` at line 104 `protected` should precede `abstract`:

```
104  abstract protected F createInstance(String pattern, TimeZone
     timeZone, Locale locale);
```

So correct it and save the file.

```
104  protected abstract F createInstance(String pattern, TimeZone
     timeZone, Locale locale);
```

Correctness - Repeated conditional tests

The **Correctness - Repeated conditional tests** violation means there are unnecessary conditionals that were already resolved earlier. The Sonar source viewer highlights the source file at line 327 by highlighting the conditional:

```
327        if (!Token.containsTokenWithValue(tokens, y) && years !=
           0) {
               while (years != 0) {
                   months += 12 * years;
                   years = 0;
               }
           }
```

The `years != 0` check at line 327 is unnecessary, since it is checked by the `while` loop too. We can safely remove the check and reduce the complexity of the `if` conditional. The block becomes:

```
327        if (!Token.containsTokenWithValue(tokens, y)) {
               while (years != 0) {
                   months += 12 * years;
                   years = 0;
               }
           }
```

Having eliminated the violations, we are ready to apply a version change to the project. Sonar will catch the change and trigger a version change event, which will appear in the **Time Machine** component.

 Of course, in a real case scenario such edits would not justify a version change but would be incorporated in the same SNAPSHOT build.

Creating your first analysis event

Locate and edit the pom.xml file inside the $COMMONS_LANG directory. In the beginning of the file, find the following line:

```
<version>3.1-SNAPSHOT</version>
```

Change it to:

```
<version>3.1.1-SNAPSHOT</version>
```

Then save the file.

Then, repackage the project and execute a Sonar analysis with:

```
$ mvn package
$ mvn sonar:sonar
```

Getting visual feedback

When the analysis is complete, visit the commons-lang dashboard to review changes. Select the previous analysis from the drop-down list at the top of the dashboard to display the difference between the current and the previous analysis.

Violations dropped by a total of **19 — Major (-2)**, **Minor (-9)**, and **Info (-8)**. Additionally, the version change now appears at the top of the **Events** widget as the latest event. This event will now appear on all historical Sonar components.

What was not planned was the minor drop of complexity per file by 0.1 percent. Indeed, it was unexpected that eliminating a few violations would even touch complexity given the size of the project—weighing at 20,000 lines—but still. This is the most rewarding part of the whole process.

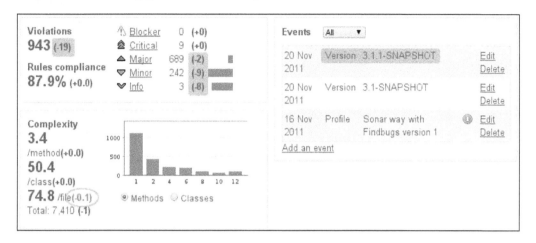

Summary

In this chapter, we covered all three methods that the Sonar platform offers to analyze projects such as Maven, Ant, and Java Runners. We configured the Sonar server and its MySQL database to accept remote connections, and installed and configured the Maven and Ant build tools. To test the set up, we downloaded and imported some popular open source libraries into Sonar for Sonar inspection.

With some projects already analyzed, we went through the Sonar web interface from the home page, down to components and project dashboard. We created a custom filter to help us track lack of test coverage across all projects and further customized the dashboard by adding widgets and rearranging the layout. Towards the end of the chapter, we eliminated a couple of violations and triggered a version change event. After a fresh analysis, we browsed to Sonar again to get visual feedback on the aforementioned changes.

In the next chapter, we will focus on coding standards, the rules that enforce them, and how to use Sonar to effectively track and eliminate them.

4
Following Coding Standards

In this chapter, we will discuss coding standards and the way Sonar monitors such violations. We will use Sonar to track down coding standards violations and correct them. To better understand the process, a small project containing classes lacking in standards department will be inspected by Sonar. Then, we will go over identifying and eliminating the violations one by one, examining the cause of each violation and providing a possible solution on how to eliminate it or overcome it. To fine grain Sonar output, we will define a custom profile focused on coding standards violations.

Before diving into the whole process, a general discussion about coding standards is necessary, exploring the purpose they serve, and why projects need to follow them and respect them at one point or another. Then, we will take a closer look at what a Sonar Rule is, how it correlates to Violations and Levels, and the Rules Compliance Metric. Under certain circumstances, some rules may not apply, triggering false positives. We will explore a couple of false positive cases and disable some rules not be taken into account by Sonar when aggregating results to produce the Rules Compliance measure. In other words, such rules should not affect project quality at all.

In this chapter we cover:

- A brief overview of coding standards and conventions
- Sonar profiles, rules, and violations
- Managing quality profiles
- Managing rules
- Creating a coding standards profile
- Inspecting violations with the radiator component
- Watching the quality improving

A brief overview of coding standards and conventions

Coding standards are defined by sets of rules governing programming style for a particular programming language. Although they differ from language to language, the objective is the same—to provide consistent, clean, readable code. Of course, development teams have different requirements and develop their own rule sets customized to their own preferences and programming habits. However, while the coding standards matter is subjective, the goal remains the same and many common rules apply to all projects among different programming languages.

Standards were not invented and simply handed to programmers. They matured through time, following programming languages' evolution and needs. Each language features its own standards and idioms, growing and being revised along with the language. Standards and conventions do not touch how features are designed or implemented but how they are presented to the coder. Clean-cut code often means error-free code because information and structure is more apparent to the developer. Badly written/structured code, apart from slowing the development process, discourages new developers who have to not only fight and comprehend a wall of lines and random notations but to add to this mess their own. Provide them with tight and clean code and watch them easily adjust and improve.

> Following coding conventions through your project's code base should not be considered as an add-on or a luxury. Follow some common guidelines and development will become more pleasant and effective.
>
> Software, during its lifetime, is not maintained by the original author. Standards allow developers to understand code more quickly.

In other words, from the moment your software project starts following some standards and common conventions, it will gradually become immune to non-standard writings, since most developers tend to respect other peoples' sources and try to provide quality at the same levels.

Moreover, coding conventions enable a more accurate static analysis of the code for reasons other than compiling. For example, counting the number of lines/statements or generating source code documentation, either with the *javadoc* tool or third-party software such as *Doxygen*, available at http://www.stack.nl/~dimitri/doxygen/.

Java standards

Java features a thorough set of standards across its specification covering organization and presentation aspects:

- Naming conventions
- Class and variables declarations
- Statements: methods, loops, conditionals
- Layout: indentation and white space

Sonar platform integrates rules covering all of the preceding areas. The default *Sonar Way* profile does include Java standards rules but for a more comprehensive inspection, *Sonar Way with Findbugs* is recommended. Sonar uses three separate source code analyzers, all of which feature rules on coding standards. However, *Checkstyle* is dedicated to standards' inspection, covering almost everything from common rules to right curls indentation and parameters padding.

Next, we will learn how to manage Sonar Quality Profiles and create a new one covering coding standards issues and examine how Sonar rules are defined and configured. Knowing how Sonar rules work enables us to create very specialized quality profiles, which in turn act as filters on quality axes.

Sonar profiles, rules, and violations

Sonar validates source code against a quality profile. Based on profile settings, the source code analyzers take turns parsing code and apply numerous rules. When a rule is broken, a violation is created, but what is a rule and how does it correlate to the overall quality?

Each Sonar profile consists of a collection of rules. Think of these rules as constraints to your source code. Each time Sonar parses, your code checks whether a rule is followed or not. In case the rule's criteria are not met, a new violation is created at a predefined *Severity*. The severity or level of the violation is a weighted value that affects overall quality of the **Rules Compliance Index (RCI)**.

The Rules Compliance Index

We have already talked about the RCI and now it is time to take a closer look at how it is calculated in practice. Sonar features a total of five different Severity Levels with their respective multiplier values:

Sonar Severity Levels	
Severity Level	**Severity Value (Weight)**
Blocker	5
Critical	4
Major	3
Minor	2
Info	1

For example, four violations of Minor severity would produce a total Violations' value of 8 based on the following formula:

*SeverityValue * TotalNumberofViolations = ViolationValue*

Or

2 * 4 = 8

Now assume a project of 15,000 lines with the following violation to severity levels distribution:

Total LOC: 15,000			
No. Violations	**Severity Level**	**Weight (Severity Cost)**	**Weighted Value**
0	Blocker	5	0
9	Critical	4	36
543	Major	3	1629
241	Minor	2	482
18	Info	1	18
Total Weighted Value			2165

Therefore, the project of 15,000 lines has violations at a weighted cost of 2,165 and converting this to percentage values:

$$\frac{2{,}165}{15{,}000} * 100 = 14.433$$

As you might have guessed the RCI value equals to:

$RCI = 100 - 14.43 = 85.56$

This is the total quality of the project at a nice high of 85.56 percent. The following is the consolidated formula:

$$RCI = 100 - \left(\frac{weightedviolations}{linesofcode} * 100 \right) \text{ percent}$$

A lot of thought has been put into severity levels and their respective values in order to produce accurate and representative results. Obviously, it is more efficient to spend time and energy eliminating high-level violations, which have the most impact on quality.

Managing quality profiles

Sonar comes with three predefined profiles—they are not editable but you can use them as a basis for a new custom one. Go to **Configuration** from the top of the page and then click **Quality Profiles** on the left.

Java profiles					Create
Name	Rules	Alerts	Projects	Default	Operations
Sonar way	115	0	0	Set as default	Copy
Sonar way with Findbugs	490	0		✓	Copy
Sun checks	59	0	0	Set as default	Copy

You can select the default quality profile, copy an existing one and use it as a template for a custom profile, or create a new one from scratch.

Creating a profile

Throughout the book, we will create a new *Packt profile* from scratch, adding rules chapter by chapter. By the end of the book, you will have configured a complete professional profile and have a deep understanding of the most common and important rules the platform offers. From that point on, you will be able to adjust or create numerous profiles customized down to the finest detail.

To create a new quality profile, click the **Create** link from the main profile management screen. Sonar will prompt for a profile **Name**; name it under *Packt profile* and click on the **Create Java Profile** button to save it. A new empty profile has been created.

Profile inheritance

Notice that the Sonar platform allows **profile inheritance**, minimizing profile management and modification. Inherit from a base profile and modify according to your needs.

Associating projects to profiles

Click on a profile's **Name** and then the **Projects** tab to view a list of associated projects with that profile. From here, you can specifically associate a project to the selected profile, otherwise unassociated projects will be analyzed by the default one.

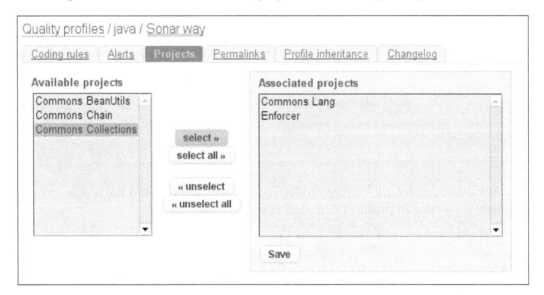

Managing rules

Click on **Packt profile** from the profile management screen to browse to the main configuration screen. Currently, the profile is empty, thus not containing any rules. The **Coding Rules** tab section features three list boxes from which you can filter rules by Analyzer Plugin, severity level, and whether the rule is activated or not.

- Plugin: Select one of the available Sonar analyzers
- Severity filter rules by severity level (Info, Minor, Major, Critical, Blocker)
- Select active, inactive, or all rules the current plugin analyzer supports

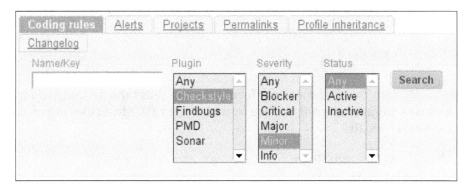

For now, select any rules of minor severity for the Checkstyle plugin and click on the **Search** button. Wait for the page to refresh and a complete list of all Checkstyle rules will render. All rules are currently deactivated and checkboxes on the left are deselected.

Adding a rule

To add the rule to the profile, simply check the Ajax checkbox on the left. There is no need to do anything more and the rule has been added. From the top right of the rules list you can **Bulk Change** rules by either activating or de-activating them all at once. Clicking on the rule's name opens up a configuration panel.

Configuring a rule

Now scroll down the list and locate the **Constant Name** Rule. Add it to the profile and click on its name to review the configuration settings:

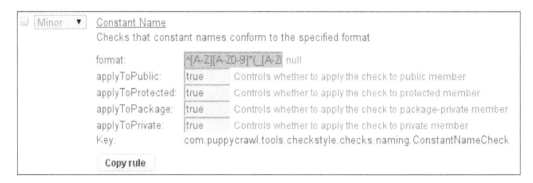

The most important part is the severity level. You can select the desired level from the drop-down menu on the left and the format of the rule. Most rules in Sonar come in three general formats:

- Regular expression rules
- Boolean `true`/`false` values
- Token/numeric values

Each rule's implementation logic uses these predetermined token values or regular expressions to decide whether to raise a violation or not at the given severity level, thus raising the total severity cost.

Regular expressions

The evaluation expression for the *Constant Name* rule reads:

```
^[A-Z][A-Z0-9]*(_[A-Z0-9]+)*$
```

This means that constant names should start with a letter and consist only of uppercase letters and numbers with words separated by an underscore, for example:

```
static MARGIN_TOP_50
```

If we want to raise a violation when a constant name contains a number, we would alter the preceding expression as follows:

```
^[A-Z]*(_[A-Z]+)*$
```

Boolean expressions

Expand the Checkstyle **Member name** rule to view its configuration panel. The regular expression checks the field's name against Java standards and the Boolean expressions control to what extent the rule will apply (private, protected, public members, and so on).

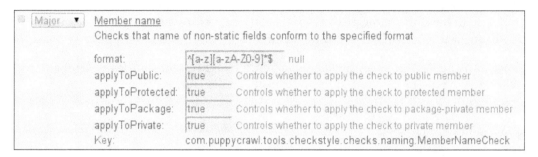

Token and value-based rules

The *Line Length* rule (Checkstyle: Major) checks for the maximum length and registers a violation if it is exceeded. However, it can be configured to your liking by adjusting the maximum line length, the number of expanded spaces for tab characters, and an optional ignore expression pattern. Lines that match this pattern will be ignored no matter how long they are.

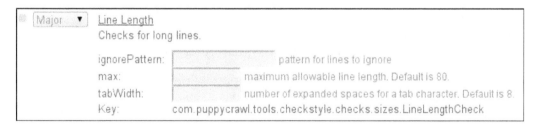

 Review your IDE settings and make sure that the maximum line length is in sync with the *Line Length* rule. If not, adjust accordingly.

Backing up and restoring profiles

To transfer or share quality profile configurations among different Sonar instances, you can **Backup** a source configuration in XML format and restore it to any target instance by clicking on the **Restore** link from the profile management screen. Select the XML source configuration file exported earlier and click on **Restore profile** to upload the file. Sonar will parse the XML and create a new identical profile. If a profile with the same name already exists, delete it before restoring. To back up a profile to XML, click on the **Backup** button.

From the same screen, it is possible to compare two different profiles and get an overview on how much they differ in respect to rules composition.

Creating a coding standards profile

To create a coding standards profile, it is necessary to know the responsibilities and specialization of each code analyzer, along with the rules it incorporates.

Sonar's source code analyzers have different responsibilities. There are some overlapping rules, but in general each analyzer has a separate focus. At the time of writing, Checkstyle has 122 rules, mainly checking Java standards and conventions.

Findbugs features 384 rules grouped by category. It specializes in locating vulnerable code that could lead to potential bugs or defects.

Findbugs Rules Breakdown	
Category	**Count**
Bad Practice	77
Correctness	139
Multithreaded Correctness	41
Dodgy	58
Experimental	10

Findbugs Rules Breakdown	
Category	**Count**
Malicious code vulnerability	12
Performance	26
Security	9
Other	12
Total	384

From the **Coding Rules** tab, you can use the **Name/Key** to filter your search. For example, you can set the **Name/Key** value to *correctness* and filter all Correctness and Multithreaded Correctness rules.

PMD comes with a total of 224 rules distributed among all quality axes such as complexity, potential bugs, and standards.

Sonar's own analyzer consists of 12 rules and focuses on complexity. One rule that is worth mentioning is the *Avoid use of //NOSONAR marker* rule. Quoting the rule's definition:

> *Any violation to quality rule can be deactivated with the //NOSONAR marker. This marker is pretty useful to exclude false-positive results but sometimes it can abusively be used to hide real quality flaws.*
>
> *This rule allows to track and/or forbid use of this marker.*

During the source code parsing process, whenever Sonar reaches a line containing an inline //NOSONAR comment, it will ignore it. For example, the following violation will be ignored:

```
if (true) {   //NOSONAR
    ...
}
```

Without the //NOSONAR tag, Sonar would normally produce a violation because the if condition defaults to true.

Selecting the rules

What rules are we going to include in our new profile? Assume a total Severity cost valued at 100. We are going to spend this total among the most common rules on coding standards and we will follow this process for the rest of the book in order to create a fairly balanced profile equal in all aspects.

To give you an idea of how it will turn out, here is a table presenting the cost-based breakdown:

Coding Standards Profile Distribution		
Severity	Rules Count	Cost
Info	5	5
Minor	8	16
Major	25	75
Critical	1	4
Blocker	0	0
Total Cost		100

That's a total of 39 rules with a Severity cost of 100. Rules have been grouped into three general categories for profile design needs:

- Naming conventions and declarations
- Basic standards
- Code layout and indentation

Add the rules presented in the following sections to the *Packt profile* we created earlier by selecting the checkbox on the left of each rule.

Do not change the severity level, and add **Avoid use of //NOSNAR marker** from the Sonar analyzer.

Naming conventions and declarations rules

Naming conventions and declarations rules are sorted from lower to higher severity in the following listing. Next, we will provide some examples for some of the rules as to exactly understand how a violation is generated and what to do in order to eliminate it.

Naming Conventions and Declarations		
Severity	Name	Analyzer
Info	Declaration Order	Checkstyle
Minor	Constant Name	Checkstyle
Minor	Naming - Avoid dollar signs	PMD
Major	Abstract Class Name	Checkstyle

Naming Conventions and Declarations		
Severity	Name	Analyzer
Major	Local Variable Name	Checkstyle
Major	Final Variable Name	Checkstyle
Major	Static Variable Name	Checkstyle
Major	Member Name	Checkstyle
Major	Method Name	Checkstyle
Major	Parameter Name	Checkstyle
Major	Multiple Variable Declarations	Checkstyle
Major	Local Home Naming	PMD
Major	Long Variable	PMD
Major	Naming - Avoid field name matching method name	PMD
Major	Naming - Class naming conventions	PMD
Major	Naming - Method naming conventions	PMD
Major	Naming - Variable naming conventions	PMD
Major	Naming - Short method name	PMD
Major	Short Variable	PMD
Critical	Naming - Suspicious equals method name	PMD

Declaration order

According to the rule's description:

Checks that the parts of a class or interface declaration appear in the order suggested by the code convention for the Java Programming Language:

- Class (static) variables: First the public class variables, next protected, then package level (no access modifier), and then private
- Instance variables: First the public class variables, next protected, then package level (no access modifier), and then private
- Constructors
- Methods

To better illustrate the specification, the following is an exemplary `Foo` class:

```
package com.packt.arapidhs;

public class DeclarationOrder {

    /**
     * <p>
     * Order static variables first
     *     <ul>
```

```
 *       <li>public</li>
 *       <li>protected</li>
 *       <li>no access</li>
 *       <li>private</li>
 *   </ul>
 * </p>
 */
public static String FOO;
protected  static String BAR;
static String FOO_BAR;
private static String BAR_FOO;

/**
 * <p>Order instance variables.</p>
 */
public String boo;
protected  String far;
String boo_far;
private String far_boo;

/** Default empty constructor. */
public Foo(){
    //
}

/* Order static methods.*/

public static void foo(){
    //
}

protected static void bar(){
    //
}

static void fooBar(){
    //
}

private static void barFoo(){
    //
}
```

```
/* Order instance methods.*/

    public void boo(){
        //
    }

    protected void far(){
        //
    }

    void booFar(){
        //
    }

    private void farBoo(){
        //
    }
}
```

This structure is all you need to know in order to lay out a Java class according to the specification. Usually, developers look at the top of the class for static and constant variables and move to the bottom to find more restricted fields and methods, moving from public down to private access.

Abstract class name

In Java, abstract classes have to start with the Abstract keyword, for example AbstractResource. The rule identifies wrongly named abstract classes using the following regular expression:

```
^Abstract.*$|^.*Factory$
```

What about the Factory part? This means that abstract classes ending with the Factory keyword do not require the Abstract prefix. So the AbstractResource and ResourceFactory class names are both valid names for abstract classes.

Variable, parameter, and method names

All variables except constants, parameters, and methods follow a simple rule. The first letter is in lower case, words inside a declaration start with an uppercase letter:

- String foo;
- String fooBar;
- void foo();

- void fooBar();

- void foo(String foo)

- void foo(String fooBar)

All these declarations are valid. Sonar checks this naming convention with the following regular expression:

```
^[a-z][a-zA-Z0-9]*$
```

Constant names

Remember that constant names are all uppercase letters and words are separated with an underscore, for example FOO or FOO_BAR.

Multiple variable declarations

This rule ensures that each variable is declared in its own statement and on its own line. Some developers have the habit of declaring many variables in one statement at once but this degrades readability.

```
String foo, bar, fooBar;
```

Becomes:

```
String foo;
String bar;
String fooBar;
```

Local home naming

Local session EJB interfaces extending the javax.ejb.EJBLocalHome interface should be suffixed by the LocalHome keyword as follows:

```
public interface HelloLocalHome extends EJBLocalHome {
 public HelloLocal create() throws CreateException;

}
```

Variable lengths

The *Long Variable* and *Short Variable* rules detect the length of a variable or a parameter and report accordingly. If a variable's length is less than three or greater than 17, then a violation is registered.

The *Naming - Short method name* is similar but applies to method names.

Naming - Avoid field name matching method name

Similar names for methods and variables prove to be confusing. This rule detects such naming patterns and reports violations. The following class declaration would violate this rule:

```
public class Foo {

  String bar;

  void bar() {
  }
```

Naming - Suspicious equals method name

The `equals` method is very important in Java language because it is used to compare and identify equal objects. When it is overridden, the method's signature should be identical to the inherited one; otherwise, equality will not work as expected.

A very common mistake is to declare the parameter as a `String` and not an object. Sonar identifies the following method declaration assuming that the developer wanted to override the `equals` method:

```
public class Foo {

  public int equals(Object o) {
  // oops, this probably was supposed to be boolean equals
  }

  public boolean equals(String s) {
  // oops, this probably was supposed to be equals(Object)
  }
}
```

The correct method would be:

```
public boolean equals(Object obj) {
  //
  }
```

Standards rules

In this section, we will discuss the second set of rules that we are going to add to the *Packt profile*:

Standards and Practice Rules		
Severity	**Name**	**Analyzer**
Info	Unused Imports	Checkstyle
Info	Unnecessary Final Modifier	PMD
Info	Unused Modifier	Checkstyle
Minor	Magic Number	Checkstyle
Major	Final Class	Checkstyle
Major	Missing Constructor	Checkstyle
Major	Assignment in Operand	PMD
Major	Abstract class without any methods	PMD

Unused imports

Leaving unused imports in a class simply clutters the file. Fortunately, modern IDEs have functions to detect and automatically remove them. This rule triggers a violation in case some of them have been forgotten.

Unnecessary final modifier

When a class is declared `final`, this means that inheritance is not allowed and so methods cannot be overridden in any way. Obviously, declaring a method `final` is not necessary and the following code would cause a violation:

```
public final class Foo {

  final void bar() {
   //
   }

}
```

Unused modifier

From the rule's definition:

Fields in interfaces are automatically public static final, and methods are public abstract. Classes or interfaces nested in an interface are automatically public and static (all nested interfaces are automatically static). For historical reasons, modifiers which are implied by the context are accepted by the compiler, but are superfluous.

And the following code:

```
public interface Foo {

public void bar();
  }


  }
```

Becomes:

```
public interface Foo {

void bar();
  }


  }
```

Magic number

According to this rule, all references to numbers apart from -1, 0, 1, and 2 cause a violation. The meaning of this rule is that when you have to change this value, change it only in one place, where the number's variable is declared and not all over the place.

What you can do is create a static `MagicNumber` class and hold numbers there or declare them as constants in the class:

```
public interface Foo {

  public void bar( int input);
    return input * 20;
  }


  }
```

Declare number 20 as a FACTOR constant variable inside the FOO class. Additionally, make it public so other classes can access it referring Foo.FACTOR:

```
public interface Foo {

public static int FACTOR = 20;

  public int bar( int input );
    return input * FACTOR;
  }


}
```

Final class

A class that has only private constructors should be declared as private because the private constructor prevents inheritance anyway. For example:

```
public final class Foo {

    /* Default private constructor */
    private Foo(){
        //
    }
}
```

Missing constructor

This rule checks that classes (except abstract ones) define a constructor and don't rely on the default one.

Abstract class without any methods

If a class does not contain any methods, thus not providing functionality but only members, it is probable that it plays the role of a Container. It is better not to instantiate such classes. To prevent instantiation, a private or a protected constructor should exist, as shown in the following code:

```
public abstract class AbstractFooBar {

    private String foo;

    private int bar;

    /* Default private constructor */
```

```
private FooBar(){
    //
}
```
}

Code layout and indentation

Finally, add rules that check code layout and whitespace:

Standards and Practice Rules

Severity	Name	Analyzer
Minor	Avoid Inline Conditionals	Checkstyle
Minor	Left Curly	Checkstyle
Minor	Paren Pad	Checkstyle
Minor	Whitespace Around	Checkstyle
Minor	Trailing Comment	Checkstyle
Major	Line Length	Checkstyle
Major	Multiple String Literals	Checkstyle
Major	For Loops Must Use Braces	PMD
Major	While Loops Must Use Braces	PMD
Major	If Else Stmts Must Use Braces	PMD

Avoid inline conditionals

Inline conditionals are essentially `if else` statements expressed in one line. While they make efficient use of text, space prove to be difficult to read. This rule detects such one liners and raises violations.

Thus the following one liner:

```
max = (a > b) ? a : b;
```

Has to be rewritten in its clearer full form as follows:

```
if (a > b) {
   max = a;
}
else {
   max = b;
}
```

Left Curly

Checkstyle's definition for the Left Curly rule states:

> *Checks for the placement of left curly braces for code blocks. The policy to verify is specified using property option. Policies eol and nlow take into account property maxLineLength.*

You can configure this rule to your liking, since the left curl placement has proved to be a very subjective matter, by selecting the appropriate policy:

- **eol** (end of line): Brace must always be placed at the end of the line.
- **nl** (new line): Brace must always be placed at the start of a new line.
- **nlow** (new line on wrap): If the line's length allows to fit on one line, then the brace must be placed at the end of the line. Otherwise, the line is wrapped and the brace is placed at the start of a new line.

Configure your IDE to lay out braces in sync with the above configuration.

Paren Pad

The Paren Pad rules check the padding of parentheses, that is, whether a space is required after a left parenthesis and before a right parenthesis.

Unpadded statement:

```
int result = (a + b) *c
```

Padded statement:

```
int result = ( a + b )   *c
```

Trailing comment

A comment is trailing when it is on the same line as a statement. This rule ensures that all comments are on separate lines.

For example:

```
int result = (a + b) *c //calculates final result
```

Becomes:

```
// calculates final result
int result = (a + b) *c
```

Multiple String literals

This rules checks whether a String literal occurs in multiple places within a single file. This is a form of code duplication and renders code maintenance quite difficult. Imagine having to replace a String literal appearing multiple times in a large file all over the place.

A better tactic is to define a constant and when a change is required, just redefine the constant.

For example:

```
public final class FooBar {

    /* Default private constructor */
    private Foo(){
        //
    }

  public String getFoo(){
    return "foo";
  }

  public String addBar(){
    return "foo" + "bar";
  }

  }
```

Would be rewritten as:

```
public final class FooBar {

  static String FOO = "foo";

    /* Default private constructor */
    private Foo(){
        //
    }

  public String getFoo(){
    return FOO;
  }

  public String addBar(){
    return FOO + "bar";
  }

  }
```

The for loops must use braces

This is same as the *Inline Conditionals* rule only for `for` loops.

PMD's example is self-explanatory:

```
for ( int i=0; i<42; i++ ) foo();
```

Should be:

```
for ( int i=0; i<42; i++ ) {

  foo();

}
```

Rules *While Loops Must Use Braces* and *If Else Stmts Must Use Braces* recommend exactly the same practice.

Inspecting violations with the Radiator component

The Radiator component is very similar to the treemap one, with three main differences:

- It is bigger—expands to full screen
- Left-click drills down to class level, eventually opening the sonar source viewer
- Right-click drills up

In treemap, you only drill down one level and it redirects you to the dashboard.

 Before installing the plugin, you can associate one of your projects to the coding standards profile we just created and perform a Sonar analysis. Then you may examine your project with the Radiator component.

Installing the Radiator plugin

Log in as an administrator and click on **Configuration** from the top and go to **SYSTEM | Update Center** from the left navigation menu. Click on the **Available Plugins** tab and scroll to the bottom until you reach the **Visualization/Reporting** section.

Visualization/Reporting	
Motion Chart	Display how a set of metrics evolves over time (requires an internet access).
PDF Report	Sonar plugin for PDF reporting
Radiator	Display measures in a big treemap.
	License: GNU LGPL 3
	Author: SonarSource
	Links: Homepage Issue Tracker
	Version: 1.1 (Feb 25, 2011)
	Install
Timeline	Advanced time machine chart (requires an internet access).

Click install and wait for Sonar to notify you that it is ready to install the plugin and you need to restart the server for the installation process to take place.

Now, to review how your project measures in the Rules Compliance department, click on **Radiator** on the left of the project's dashboard.

The radiator widget

The radiator can be also added directly to the project dashboard as a widget. Click **Configure Widget** from the dashboard screen, locate the radiator, and click on **Add Widget**.

The following screen shows what JDK 7 looks like (size is for LOC and color for **Rules compliance**):

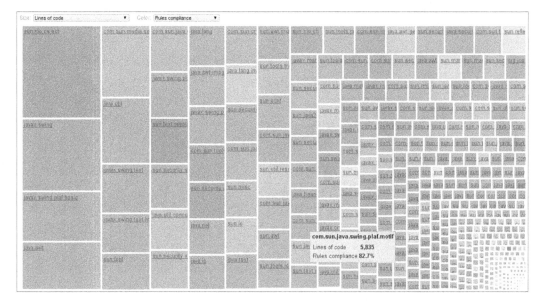

Mouse over a box to view the exact RCI percentage or click on it to drill down one level from project to package and so on. SonarSource hosts the complete JDK7, so you can watch a live demonstration at `http://nemo.sonarsource.org/`.

Basically, you:

1. Drill down to class level using the radiator.
2. Identify the packages lacking in coding standards.
3. Drill to class level—click the box to open the source viewer.
4. Identify violations and correct them.
5. Run a Sonar analysis again to review the results.

Watch the quality improving

To closely monitor how the RCI metrics fluctuate during development along with the Violations count and Lines of Code, you can add the *Timeline* widget to the dashboard. Navigate to the dashboard and click on the **Configure Widgets** link. If the Timeline widget is not present, select it from the upper yellowish panel by clicking on **Add Widget**.

Configuring the Timeline widget

In edit mode, select the **Edit** link from the widget's header bar and name it as `Coding Standards` and for the three metric values select:

- **Lines of code**
- **Rules compliance**
- **Violations**

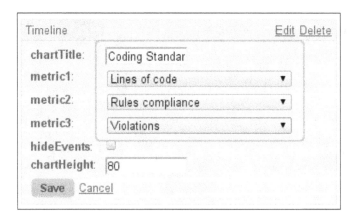

Click on **Save** and **Back to the dashboard** from the top to return to view mode.

The following is the *Timeline* widget in action:

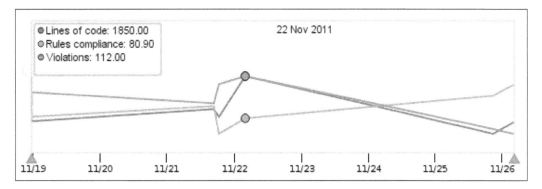

Summary

In this chapter, we reviewed Java coding standards and conventions, and the way Sonar applies them to your source code. We went through the process of creating a new cost-based quality profile detailing rules configuration. Finally, we installed the Radiator plugin from Sonar's update center and configured the Timeline widget on the project dashboard.

In the next chapter, we will discuss Sonar code reviews and how they can contribute to a project's lifecycle. We will further explore some of the visual components Sonar offers and enable reporting capabilities.

5
Managing Measures and Getting Feedback

In this chapter, we will discuss code reviews, how they are beneficial to development teams, and what the Sonar platform can do to ease the review process. Next, we will configure the notification system to subscribe to code review events registered and raised by Sonar.

Having already detailed violations, it is time to introduce metric thresholds to better control quality and custom measures. While calculated metrics exist in abundance within the platform, there are business measures that are not applicable in an automated process. Custom measures help extend information and cover this aspect too. Finally, we will continue our journey through the platform's visual components, such as the *Timeline* and *Motion Chart*, along with *PDF* reporting capabilities.

In this chapter, we cover:

- Reviewing code
- Sonar manual reviews
- Configuring notifications
- Defining metric thresholds and alerts
- Sonar manual measures
- Quality reporting on your project
- Getting visual feedback

Reviewing code

Writing code is not a monolithic procedure and is never written once. At least a couple of revisions take place before we consider it to be final. Of course, when a bug arises we are forced to revise and correct or improve the code but it is best to code and develop pro-actively. Adding code reviews as an additional process before committing code helps identify problematic areas early and ensure better quality. As a matter of fact, we could say that the Sonar platform reviews code from many perspectives, generating results over different axes. But systematic examination and code inspection by team developers is irreplaceable.

To quote Eric S. Raymond's Linus's Law named in honor of Linus Torvalds:

Linus's Law:

> *Given enough eyeballs, all bugs are shallow.*

The most common ways to perform code reviews are:

- Via e-mail communication: Report on code expecting to hear back
- Pair programming: The developers work closely together
- Software Managed Reviews: Use tools to streamline the process

The review process using specifically designed software is very similar to maintaining and using a bug tracking system. Instead of bugs, developers assign and are assigned code reviews. A code review does not necessarily mean code changes. The point is to begin a discussion of why something is written the way it is, whether there is room for improvement, and what the alternatives are. There will be cases where the code author has real reasons and needs to code things in a specific way, but this is not always the case. A more experienced developer may foresee hidden bugs and dangerous cases not covered in code, requiring changes.

Code reviews do not only help to improve code and quality but educate the developers too. Less experienced developers gain insight on good practices and techniques from their colleagues. Additionally, it is often a good idea to let new developers review others' code straight away. Exposing them to source code and in-house libraries early will help them integrate better with the team and adopt a similar programming style. Finally, when developers know beforehand that their code will get reviewed, they tend to be more careful and supply better documentation in order to assist the reviewer.

The Sonar platform features code reviews management complementing the automatically calculated metrics produced by the separate analyzers; thus we have both machine and developer feedback in one single place.

Sonar manual reviews

Similar to Bug Tracking systems, reviews are assigned to users and may have one of four possible statuses:

- **Open**: The initial status
- **Resolved**: Mark the violation as resolved
- **Reopened**: Reopen the violation for review
- **Closed**: Automatic as long as the violation has been resolved

Initially the review is in the Open status. When code changes resolve, the violation referenced by the review is marked as resolved and closed automatically. If the same violation takes place again, Sonar reopens the review again.

If you do not intend to resolve the violation or you believe it does not qualify as a violation, you can resolve it by flagging it as **False-Positive**.

Assigning reviews

First of all, drill down to the Java class level and open the source code with Sonar Source Viewer by clicking on the class name. You can use the treemap/radiator component to drill down to class level or browse violations from the project dashboard.

When inside the Source Viewer, click on the rightmost **Violations** tab to view the violated sections of the source code. Each violation has a light blue header with the level and name. Move your mouse over the header to make the **Review** and **Flag as false-positive** links appear.

 You must be logged in and have the **Users** role to be able to assign reviews.

Locate the violation you want to review and click on the **Review** link. Enter review details in the text area that opens and fill in the **Assignee** name – start typing a username and a filtered list will pop up. When you are done, click on the **Add Comment** button. For example, take a look at the following screenshot:

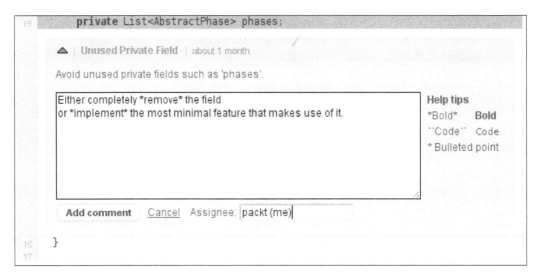

You can style your comments using special wiki style notations as seen on the right under **Help tips**. The following shows how the previous review looks:

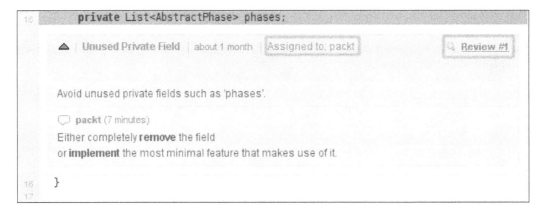

The review assignee is now visible and a new link appears on the right of the violation header named after **Review #ID**. Click on the link for additional details such as assignment date and original reporter—author. Additionally, you can manually **Resolve** the review, flag it as **False-Positive**, or **Reassign** it to a different user. In any case, the review will automatically resolve when the corresponding violation resolves too.

Browsing reviews

Sonar provides a comprehensive reviews search engine. When you log in to Sonar, click on the **Reviews** link under **Filters** from the left menu to bring up the **Reviews** browser. By default, only reviews assigned to you will display. Clear the **Assigned to** text field and click on **Search** to browse all reviews. From here, you can filter reviews by **Status**, **Violation Severity**, and of course project.

To find reviews reported by a specific user, type their name in the **Created by** field. The results list, which appears below the search panel, is clickable and transfers you to a more detailed screen allowing to resolve the review or to reassign it. You can include or exclude **False-Positive** reviews by making the appropriate selection from the red highlighted select menu.

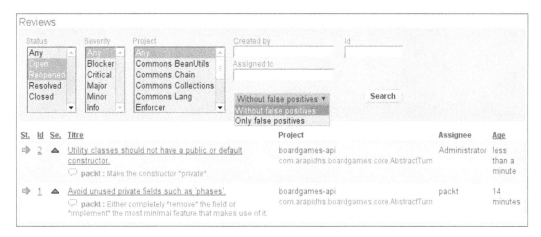

Configuring notifications

Sonar features an *e-mail notification* mechanism allowing users to subscribe to certain events. To activate notifications, you have to supply Sonar with e-mail server configuration. Log in as an administrator and go to **Configuration | General Settings | Email**.

Fill in the fields with your e-mail server configuration and click on the **Save Email Settings** button when done.

```
Email Settings

             SMTP host: [                    ]    For example "smtp.gmail.com". Leave
                                                   blank to disable email sending.

             SMTP port: [25                  ]    Port number to connect with SMTP
                                                   server.

            Use secure [No  ▼]                     Whether to use secure connection and
           connection:                            its type.

      SMTP username: [packt               ]    Optional - if you use authenticated
                                                   SMTP, enter your username.

      SMTP password: [·····               ]    Optional - as above, enter your
                                                   password if you use authenticated
                                                   SMTP.

         From address: [noreply@nowhere     ]    Emails will come from this address. For
                                                   example - "noreply@sonarsource.com".
                                                   Note that server may ignore this setting
                                                   (like does GMail).

          Email prefix: [SONAR]                 This prefix will be prepended to all
                                                   outgoing email subjects.

      [ Save Email Settings ]


Test Configuration

                   To: [packt               ]

              Subject: [Test Message from Sonar ]

              Message: [This is a test message from Sonar]
```

Users can now subscribe to notifications from their profile settings. Click on the username link located on the top bar and check the events you want to subscribe to under the **Notifications** section.

For example, you can subscribe to the reviews event and receive an e-mail whenever a *review* has been assigned or was created by you.

Defining metric thresholds and alerts

To further streamline and automate quality inspection, Sonar introduces dynamic threshold alerts by assigning threshold values to specific metrics. Whenever a metric exceeds the configured value or threshold, an alert is raised. Alerted projects are specifically marked both in the projects list and in the dashboard to indicate the threshold violation.

Each quality profile features its own separate set of alerts. Next, we will add two alerts to **Rules compliance** and **Testing Coverage**. Click on **Configuration**, go to the **Quality Profiles** page, and click on the **Packt profile** we have already created (if you haven't created it, simply create a new one by clicking on **Copy** to copy the default profile, named **Sonar way**). Then, click on the **Alerts** tab to navigate to the **Alerts** management screen.

To create an alert, we need to define:

- The metric the threshold applies to
- Compare type: **is greater than**, **is less than**, **equals**, **is not**
- The Warning alert threshold: When this is reached a **warning** alert triggers
- The Error alert threshold: When this value is reached an **error** alert triggers

Similarly, we create a **Rules compliance** alert with warning and error thresholds at **75%** and **70%** respectively and a **Coverage** one with warning and error thresholds at **75%** and **60%** respectively.

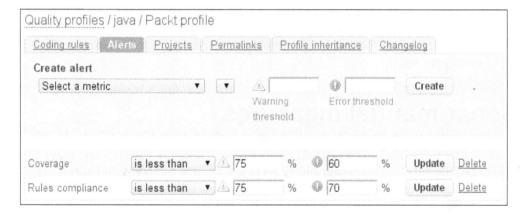

From now, projects associated with the Packt profile will trigger warning alerts when either **Coverage** or **Rules Compliance** metrics fall below **75%** and error alerts when **Coverage** metric is below **60%** or **Rules Compliance** metric is below **70%**.

Perform a new analysis and visit the dashboard. Click on the **Configure widgets** link and add **Alert** widget. Navigate to your project's directory and enter mvn sonar:sonar or ant sonar to perform a new analysis.

Next you can see how metrics that have exceeded above thresholds are highlighted in red and a notification is visible inside the dashboard. To get rid of this irritating reminder, we have to write some more tests :).

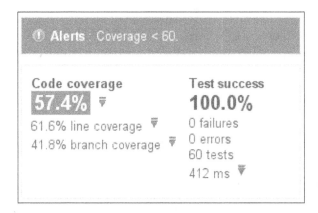

The Build Breaker

To create an even more strict development environment, you can install the Build Breaker plugin and cause the build process to fail and report as broken whenever a metric exceeds threshold values.

The plugin is available for installation from **Configuration | Update Center** under the section **Integration**. Remember to restart the server in order to complete the installation process.

Sonar manual measures

Apart from the metrics that are automatically collected during analysis, Sonar offers more flexibility by allowing us to add custom ones. There are some factors that simply cannot be calculated or automatically aggregated, such as team size, business value, or story points of the features that are to be implemented in subsequent versions. Nevertheless, such measures are necessary in order get the complete picture.

Sonar comes with three predefined custom measures. Log in as administrator or the *packt* user we have already created and go to **Configuration | Manual Metrics** to take a look at the following measures:

- **Burned Budget**: The budget already used in the project
- **Business Value**: An indication of the value of the project for the business
- **Team size**: The size of the project team

Creating the Story Points measure

Let's create a new custom measure called **Story Points**. Fill in the form on the right and click on the **Create** button when you are finished.

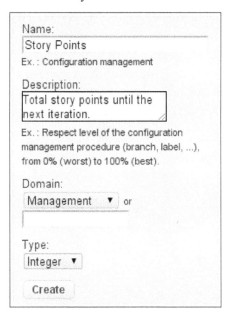

What are Story Points?

Planning Poker or Scrum Poker is a technique to estimate effort and time on features implementation. Each developer assigns Story Points to features based on how complex or difficult they are to implement. When everyone has assigned points, a discussion begins especially about features that were assigned both low and high Story Points from the team.

Finally, a consensus is reached, Story Points are decided, and the team has a better collective understanding about the features and the effort required until the next version.

The **Story Points** manual measure has been now created and is available to any project in Sonar.

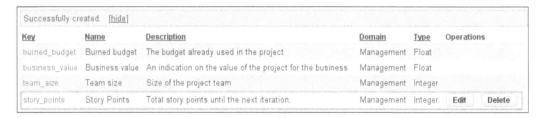

Managing manual measures

Visit the project dashboard and click on the **Manual Measures** link under the **CONFIGURATION** section.

Currently, there are no measures associated with any project. Click on the **Add Measure** link located on the top right, select the **Team Size** and **Story Points** from the menu, and enter the measure's value and description respectively.

Click on **Save** to return to the previous screen and notice that both measures are marked with an orange box as pending. An analysis is required before they become available to the dashboard. Perform an analysis and browse to the dashboard to add the Manual Measures widget.

Click on the **Configure Widgets** link from top left, locate the **Custom Measures** widget, and click on **Add Widget**. The widget initially is empty. Click on **edit** from the widget's header to add the measures you want.

If the team size changes or a new set of feature demands different story points, you can always go to the **Manual Measures** screen and edit the values accordingly.

This is how the widget will look on the dashboard:

Quality reporting on your project

Sonar offers reporting capabilities on project quality and metrics in the form of a plugin. It aggregates project dashboard information in a presentable and readable format inside a PDF document.

The plugin, developed by Antonio Martin Muniz Martin, requires Sonar Version 2.4 or higher. To get some insight about the plugin's development, you can visit Martin's blog at `http://blog.klicap.es/en/products/sonarpdfreportplugin`.

Have a look at some of the more advanced features available in the commercial version of the plugin. Sonar includes the limited but still very valuable open source version.

Installing the PDF report plugin

Log in to Sonar with administrator privileges, click on **Configuration** and then **Update Center** from the left.

Navigate to the **Available Plugins** tab and scroll down to the **Visualization/ Reporting** section.

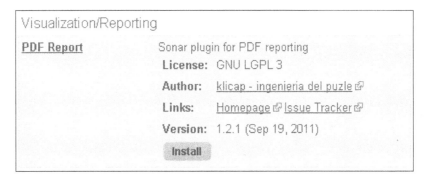

Click on **Install** to initiate the installation process and restart the Sonar server when it is complete to make the plugin available. Next, from the project's dashboard, click on the **Configure widgets** link to add the PDF report widget to the dashboard.

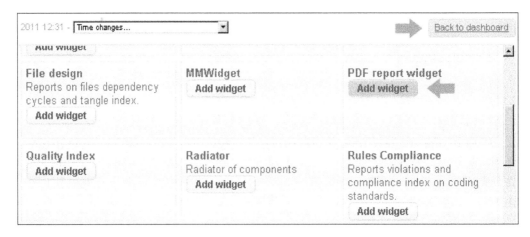

Getting the project report

The plugin generates a PDF report based on Sonar analysis results. Run a Sonar analysis by executing the Sonar Maven goal and visit the dashboard afterward to browse the results and download the fresh PDF report.

```
$ mvn sonar:sonar
```

The **PDF Report** panel in the dashboard features a **Download** link to the report's document. Click on it to download the document. If the report widget is empty and displays **No Data**, make sure that a Sonar analysis was previously executed successfully.

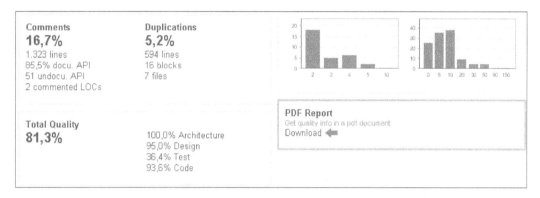

The reports consist of the following sections for each module in the project:

- **Report Overview**
- **Violations Analysis**
- **Violations Details**

Some of the notable features in the commercial version of the reporting are:

- Include timeline charts for selected metrics
- Include information provided by other external plugins
- Set a minimum-level priority for report
- Logotype customization — branding

The following are some screens of an actual PDF report. Alternatively, you can download a sample from `http://docs.codehaus.org/download/attachments/116359257/pdf-report-1.1.pdf`.

1.1. Report Overview

Static Analysis

Lines of code	Comments	Complexity
6,598	16.7%	1.8
15 packages	1,323 comment lines	6.6 /class
111 classes		730 decision points
415 methods		
5.2% duplicated lines		

Dynamic Analysis

Code Coverage	Test Success
20.5%	100.0%
56 tests	0 failures
	0 errors

Coding Rules Violations

Rules Compliance	Violations
95.3%	134

The second section of the report breaks down and counts each violation sorted by multiplicity, as shown next:

1.2. Violations Analysis

Most violated rules	
Bad practice - Class is Serializable, but doesn't define serialVersionUID	27
Magic Number	26
Non-transient non-serializable instance field in serializable class	22
Dodgy - Class implements same interface as superclass	13
Bad practice - Transient field that isn't set by deserialization.	6

Customizing the report

To produce reports for managers, it would be better to omit violations details from the document, as they do not add any further useful information to them. The PDF Report plugin comes with two layouts; *workbook* which is the default one and *executive*. To change the report type to *executive* go to **Configuration | General Settings | PDF Report** and fill in the field **Type** with the value executive as shown:

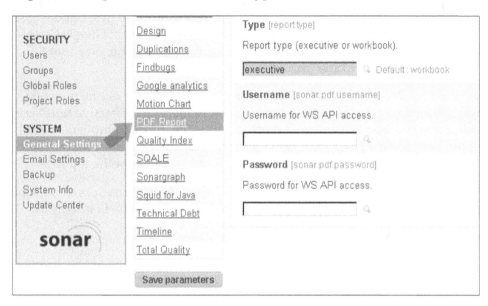

Click on the **Save parameters** button to save your changes and the next time an analysis is run, the report generated will contain only the following sections:

- Report Overview
- Violations Analysis

Getting visual feedback

Sonar offers some very interesting and modern visual components to help the developer or manager understand the progress and evolution of the code base over time:

- Motion Chart plugin
- Timeline plugin

You can find the plugins in the **Update** Center **under** the **Reporting/Visualization** section. Install them and do not forget do restart the Sonar server after the installation. Finally, run a new analysis of a project and launch your browser.

Timeline plugin

The Sonar Timeline plugin uses Google's Annotated Time Line component. It is the same component that Google uses to render trends, stock analysis, and website analytics. You can find more information about the component at Google Code (`http://code.google.com/intl/el-GR/apis/chart/interactive/docs/gallery/annotatedtimeline.html`).

To use the Timeline plugin, click on the **Timeline** link from the left menu when browsing the project dashboard. The component renders an interactive time-series chart featuring data on three default metrics: Coverage, Rules Compliance, and Lines Of Code. You can change the time scale from one day to one year or more. You can trace the lines with your mouse and review exact point values at the top left.

Project events are also flagged on the chart, so you can see when each event took place. The legend on the left of the chart reads all project events since the first analysis.

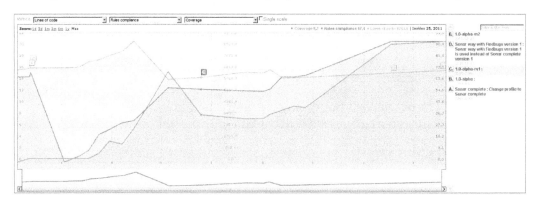

Let us zoom the previous screen to better understand what the timeline actually shows and what we can learn about the project.

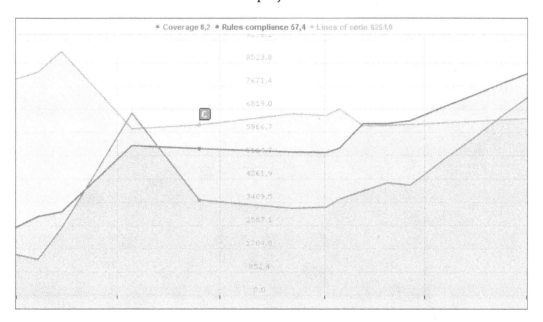

The default metrics charted are:

- **Coverage**: Bottom line (blue color)
- **Rules Compliance**: Middle line (red color)
- **Lines of code**: Top line (yellow color)

The timeline focuses on the middle five months of development. Lines of code have been greatly reduced and stabilized (refactoring) and the source code continuously improves in an effort to follow standards and conventions. The same goes for code coverage, although the major drop during the second month probably requires attention.

We can change the metrics from the select menus on the top left to cover architecture and complexity or any other aspect you desire. For example:

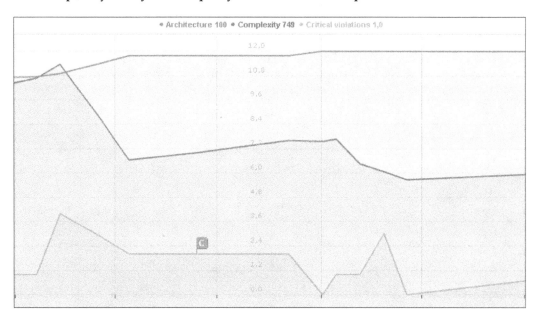

The metrics depicted are:

- **Architecture**: Top line (blue color)
- **Complexity**: Middle line (red color)
- **Critical Violations**: Bottom line (yellow color)

Complexity has almost dropped to half as a result of refactoring while **Critical Violations** have been kept at a minimum. **Architecture** gradually reached 100 percent. So we learn that the project has greatly improved in terms of source code size and complexity. There is room for improvement though in the testing and coverage department.

Motion Chart plugin

The Motion Chart plugin is the most impressive plugin available for the platform. It generates an animation of bubbles inside the chart, with each bubble representing a project module. Size and bubble color can be parameterized from a plethora of available metrics. The chart is available from the **Motion Chart** link on the left menu when browsing the project dashboard. It also offers two more renditions, such as bar chart and line chart.

Bubble chart

The following screen shows the bubble chart in action. Each bubble is a separate project module. You can toggle modules' visibility from the right-panel menu. Check the **Trails** checkbox to cause the bubbles to leave a trail while the animation plays. To start the animation, just click on the **play** button on the bottom left of the chart.

You can adjust the **Period** of the chart from the select menu on the top left in a range of one month up to two years. Uncheck the **Components** checkbox to view the project as one single bubble, leave it checked to break it down into its modules—components.

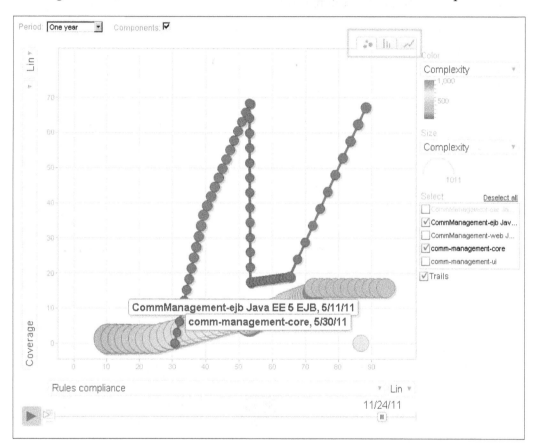

The above chart is configured as follows:

- **Complexity** (Size): Particle size is proportional to package complexity
- **Lines of code** (X axis): Total number of effective LOCs in the package excluding comments, file header, and blanks
- **Test Coverage** (Y axis): Percentage value of Unit Test Coverage

For greater effect, you can use the Color drop-down menu at the top right and map it to an additional metric.

Bar chart

Click on the second bar icon at the top right to switch to the Bar Chart mode and click on **play** to start the animation. Each bar or project module raises or lowers respectively to the metric it represents. Likewise, you can configure a metric for the color. The bars are sorted by a defined metric value too, and you can change this value from the menu on the bottom right.

For example in the following screenshot, the bars are sorted by **Lines of code** in descending order:

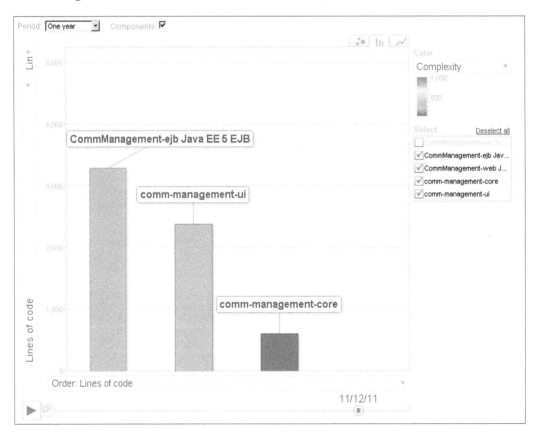

Summary

In this chapter, we went through the code review process using the Sonar platform. We configured the mail server to enable users subscribe to review events and receive e-mail, and created thresholds on **Coverage** and **Rules Compliance** metrics. Then, we covered custom measures and how we can use them to introduce new metrics into the system. We created the Story Points custom measure and added the appropriate widget to our project's dashboard. Finally, we installed Reporting and Visualization plugins such as PDF Reporting, Timeline, and Motion Chart. We detailed all three components and learned how to read and interpret the information they provide.

In the next chapter, we will discuss violations that relate to potential bugs and how best to eliminate them. We will use Sonar components to drill down to classes and filter such violations in an effort to spot them and eliminate them. The Sonar Source Viewer will prove to be an invaluable tool of great assistance and efficiency. We will use some practical examples of violated code and provide possible solutions to such violations.

6
Hunting Potential Bugs

In this chapter, we will review and detail some of the most common violations that can lead to bugs or defects—unexpected behavior. We will then add coding standards rules to complement the custom profile. Next, we will install the Violation Density plugin, an alternate overall representation of project quality. Finally, we will install the Sonar Eclipse plugin, an ultimate tool that brings Sonar measures directly to our IDE.

In this chapter we cover:

- Potential bugs violations
- Installing the Violation Density plugin
- Integrating Sonar to Eclipse

Potential bugs violations

The three Sonar analyzers feature an extensive set of rules checking code that can lead to potential bugs and deficiencies. We are going to add to the custom *Packt profile* some of the most common and important rules. So far, we have added rules for Coding Standards costing a total of 100 points. For potential bugs, we will add rules to reach the target value of 200, as it is the most important part along with complexity.

To calculate the total cost/profile value, remember that each violation has a rating from 1 to 5. The higher the value, the stricter the profile becomes. For example, adding five Critical checks would raise the value of the profile to 15.

The following table breaks down the rules we will use sorted by level. Most of these checks are implemented by the *Findbugs* analysis engine.

Potential Bugs Profile Distribution		
Severity	**Rules Count**	**Cost**
Major	25	75
Critical	25	100
Blocker	5	25
Total Cost		200

That's a total of 55 rules at a cost of 200. We tried to include important rules from all analyzers, avoiding overlapping and similar checks. We can split the rules into the following three general categories:

- Dodgy code
- Program flow
- Security issues

Next, we will present the rules in table form and further detail those that need some clarification. Log in to Sonar and add the rules to the *Packt profile* as you read. Feel free to change the severity of some rules to fit it to your needs.

Dodgy code rules

The following table shows the total 33 rules that cover dodgy code potentially leading to bugs and unexpected behavior. This category features the most rules of all three. Some of the checks identify code that will surely break while others suggest a rewrite to provide clarity and performance.

Malicious Code		
Severity	**Name**	**Analyzer**
Major	Use Notify All Instead Of Notify	PMD
Major	String Buffer Instantiation With Char	PMD
Major	Use String Buffer For String Appends	PMD
Major	Use Equals To Compare Strings	PMD
Major	Constructor Calls Overridable Method	PMD
Major	Check `ResultSet`	PMD
Major	Close `Resource`	PMD
Major	Avoid StringBuffer field	PMD

Malicious Code

Severity	Name	Analyzer
Major	Avoid Decimal Literals In Big Decimal Constructor	PMD
Major	Avoid Duplicate Literals	PMD
Major	Suspicious reference comparison to constant	Findbugs
Major	Ambiguous invocation of either an inherited or outer method	Findbugs
Major	Consider returning a zero length array rather than `null`	Findbugs
Major	Method ignores return value	Findbugs
Major	Usage of GetResource may be unsafe if class is extended	Findbugs
Major	Method ignores results of `InputStream.read()`	Findbugs
Critical	Method does not release lock on all paths	Findbugs
Critical	Code contains a hard coded reference to an absolute pathname	Findbugs
Critical	Invalid syntax for regular expression	Findbugs
Critical	Null pointer dereference	Findbugs
Critical	Nullcheck of value previously dereferenced	Findbugs
Critical	Don't use `removeAll` to clear a collection	Findbugs
Critical	Method may fail to close database resource	Findbugs
Critical	Method may fail to close stream	Findbugs
Critical	Method may fail to close database resource on exception	Findbugs
Critical	Method may fail to close stream on exception	Findbugs
Critical	Suspicious reference comparison	Findbugs
Critical	Misplaced `Null` Check	PMD
Critical	Equals Hash Code	Checkstyle
Blocker	Impossible `cast`	Findbugs
Blocker	Null value is guaranteed to be dereferenced	Findbugs
Blocker	`close()` invoked on a value that is always null	Findbugs
Blocker	`equals(...)` used to compare incompatible arrays	Findbugs

Use notifyAll instead of notify

In Java we can signal other threads to wake up using the `notify()` and `notifyAll()` methods. There is a lot of discussion on which is the most appropriate call. It all boils down to how many threads you want to notify and if there is a reason for notifying all waiting threads when a task has finished. Using `notify()`, only one monitoring thread will be notified and will be chosen by the JVM. In the case of many waiting threads, there is the slight possibility to lock out some of them. Using `notifyAll()` guarantees that all monitoring threads on the object will wake up and start running.

So using `notifyAll()`, it is a safe play and does the job whether there are many or only one thread to be notified. The trade-off is the slight performance cost for waking up threads that can't do anything anyway. If you are not sure which call to use, then always use `notifyAll()`.

There are cases where calling `notify()` makes perfect sense though. Consider the classic producer/consumer where the producer produces a packet to be consumed by only one consumer from the packet queue. There is no point in waking any more threads using `notifyAll()`. You can flag the violation as a false-positive.

StringBuffer instantiation with char

Instantiating a `StringBuffer` with `char` will not append the character to the buffer, but it will be converted to `int`, which is used to define the buffer's size. For example:

```
StringBuffer buffer = new StringBuffer('c');
```

Character c will be automatically converted into `int` and the result is used to initialize the buffer's length size. Alternatively, you can create the buffer and append the `char` or construct it using double quotes.

Use StringBuffer for String appends

When concatenating Strings using the + operator, the compiler actually uses `StringBuffer` to perform the operation. For example, the following statement:

```
String s = "foo" + "bar";
```

Compiles to:

```
StringBuffer buffer = new StringBuffer();
buffer.append("foo");
buffer.append("bar");
s = buffer.toString();
```

For simple concatenations, this is fine but inside a loop would cause a StringBuffer object to be instantiated in each iteration, wasting memory and degrading performance. Consider the following loop:

```
String s  = "";
for ( int i = 0; i < 5; i ++ ){
    s = s + String.valueOf(i);
}
```

The compiler would instantiate five objects to perform the concatenation. The preceding loop could be written as follows:

```
String s  = "";
StringBuffer buffer = new StringBUffer();
for ( int i = 0; i < 5; i ++ ){
    buffer.append(i);
}
s = buffer.toString();
```

Constructor calls overridable method

To better allow inheritance and provide a healthy framework, free of bugs, calling overridable methods in class constructors is not acceptable and can cause many problems from exceptions to inconsistent object state. Practically, this is instantiating a subclass which overrides a method called in the superclass constructor. Consider the following classes Base and Child:

```
public class Base {

   public Base(){
      printResult();
   }

   abstract void printResult();

}
```

The printResult() method to be implemented by subclasses of Base is called in the constructor.

```
public class Child extends Base {

   String result;

   public Child( final String result ){
      super();     // printResult() will be invoked
      this.result = result;
```

```
    }

    @Override
    public void printResult(){
        System.out.println(result);
    }

}
```

The `Base` constructor will invoke `printResult()` before the variable result has been finalized, thus getting a null value.

Close Resource

When opening a Connection, Statement, or a ResultSet always close the resource in a `finally` block, as shown in the following code:

```
Connection conn = openConnection();
Statement stmt = null;
String query = createQuery();

try {

    stmt = conn.createStatement();
    ResultSet rs = stmt.executeQuery(query);

} catch (){
...
} finally {

  if (rs!=null) rs.close();
  if (stmt!=null) stmt.close();
  if (conn!=null) conn.close();

}
```

Leaving open connections and result sets can very quickly exhaust the connection pool.

> Notice that `close()` calls may require further exception handling in a `try catch` block. To keep the `finally` block simple, you could create a `static` utility method to handle the closing of resources:
>
> ```
> static void close(Connection c, Statement st,
> ResultSet rs)
> ```

Ambiguous invocation of either an inherited or outer method

When you are invoking a method of an inner class and want to be resolved to the outer class implementation, use `super` to clarify this. Additionally, you can use the `this` keyword to emphasize that the inherited method is the one called, which is the default behavior nevertheless.

```
super.foo()  // outer class

this.foo()    // inner class
```

Consider returning a zero length array rather than null

Instead of returning a null reference when there are no results, it is better to return an empty array or an empty list. In this way, callers of the method will not have to check for possible `null` returns.

```
public class Department {

   private final static Employees[] NULL_EMPLOYEES = new
Employees[0];

   private Employees[] employees;

   public Employees[] retrieveEmployees(){
      ...
   }

}
```

To prevent allocating additional heap space each time a zero length array return is required, we can define a static zero length array, thus returning the same reference without allocating any more memory.

Method ignores return value

When a method is invoked on an immutable object, the object is not updated but a new one is returned. This is a very common mistake.

```
String s = "packt";
s.replace('a','i');
```

The internal state of the `String` object is not changed because the method `replace(..)` returns a new String. The correct version is to reassign the processed value as follows:

```
String s = "packt";
s = s.replace('a','i');
```

Method does not release lock on all paths

In a multithread environment, it is essential to ensure that thread locks are released upon a task's completion. Otherwise, monitors could never access the object and get locked out indefinitely. The best place to release a lock is in the `finally` block, as shown in the following code:

```
Lock lock = ...;
lock.lock();

try {

    // do something

} finally {
    lock.unlock();
}
```

Null pointer dereference

A `null` pointer dereference causes `NullPointerException` to happen at runtime, so this violation is quite important and has to be taken care of.

```
String role = user.getRole();

if (role.equals("admin")){

    ...
}
```

If the role is `null`, the highlighted code will throw `NullPointerException`. If the role variable is checked for `null` after it has been dereferenced, a *Nullcheck of value previously dereferenced* violation is triggered because the check is redundant.

Suspicious reference comparison

Another common mistake is to test objects for equality with the `==` or `!=` operators. These operators compare references and not values. Thus the `equals()` method and the `==` operator perform two different operations. The correct way to compare two objects and evaluate whether they have the same state/characteristics is to use the `equals()` method.

In the following example, the `==` operation reports that the the two `String` variables are not the same in the sense that they refer to two different objects, while the `equals()` method identifies them as equal because the values of those objects are the same.

```
Public class TestEquals {

  public static void main(String args[]) {

    String s1 = "Hello";
    String s2 = new String(s1);

    System.out.println(s1.equals(s2)); // true

    System.out.println( (s1 == s2) );   // false

  }

}
```

Misplaced null check

A misplaced null check can lead to `NullPointerException`.

```
if ( role.equals("admin") && role != null  ) {
  ..
}
```

The correct way is to place the null check in front of the `if` statement. The second part of the statement will be evaluated only if the the role variable is not `null`:

```
if ( role != null && role.equals("admin") ) {
  ..
}
```

Impossible cast

Impossible cast means that `ClassCastException` will be thrown. To better understand this violation, let's look at the following example. Suppose we have the classes `User` and `Administrator`.

```
public class User {
  ...
}

public class Administrator extends User {
  ...
}

Object obj = new Administrator();
```

The variable `obj` is an `Administrator` but also a `User` and an `Object`, so casting `obj` back to `User` and `Object`. Since `Administrator` is a subclass of `User`, the compiler has enough information to perform the casting.

However, the opposite is not necessarily true. When we do casting, we provide the compiler with a hint telling that the given object is of a specific type, but if the compiler has not enough information to perform the operation a cast exception is thrown. Casting `User` to `Administrator` will probably not work because it is higher in the inheritance tree.

 Apart from the hierarchy, another requirement to perform casting is that both classes are loaded by the same classloader.

Program flow rules

The next set of 14 rules cover code handling program flow and general exception handling violations.

Program Flow		
Severity	**Name**	**Analyzer**
Major	Do not throw exception in finally	PMD
Major	Finalize Does Not Call Super Finalize	PMD
Major	Dataflow Anomaly Analysis	PMD
Major	Avoid Calling Finalize	PMD
Major	Avoid Catching NPE	PMD
Major	Method ignores exceptional return value	Findbugs
Major	Switch statement found where default case is missing	Findbugs
Critical	Useless control flow	Findbugs
Critical	Exception created and dropped rather than thrown	Findbugs
Critical	An apparent infinite loop	Findbugs
Critical	An apparent infinite recursive loop	Findbugs
Critical	Missing `break` in `switch`	PMD
Critical	Avoid Catching `Throwable`	PMD
Critical	Method uses the same code for two branches	Findbugs

Do not throw exception in finally

Avoid throwing exceptions in the `finally` block because it might hide other more important exceptions inside the `try catch` block. For example:

```
try {

  process();

} catch () {

  handleException();

} finally {

  cleanUp();

}
```

The preceding code is valid as long as the `cleanUp()` method does not throw an exception. Otherwise, if `process` throws an exception and later in the `finally` block one more exception is thrown by the `cleanUp()` method, the second exception will bubble up hiding the more important exception thrown by the `process()` method.

A better practice would be to either handle or log all exceptions inside a `finally` block and not throw new ones.

Finalize does not call Super Finalize

All Java classes inherit the `finalize()` method from `java.lang.Object`. This method is invoked by the garbage collector when the JVM determines that the object is eligible for collecting.

When overriding `finalize()` it is a good programming practice to use a `try-catch-finally` block and always call `super.finalize()` to close all resources used by the object.

```
protected void finalize() throws Throwable {

    try {

        close();        // close connections

    } finally {

        super.finalize();
    // add more code as needed
    }

}
```

Two things about implementing the finalize() method:

- The Garbage Collector has to check the object twice: once to run the finalize() method and then check that the object was not resurrected during finalization.
- Objects with implemented finalize() methods are treated by the Garbage Collector as special cases, slowing the process of garbage collection.

Avoid calling finalize

A healthy application should not rely on explicitly invoking finalization methods and it should leave the garbage collector take care of memory clean up. To quote a fellow developer Charles Miller:

> *Java garbage collection is a very finely tuned tool.* System.gc() *is a sledge-hammer.*

Calling System.gc(), we force the garbage collector to take action but naturally the automatic invocation of the collector should suffice and optimally manage Java heap space.

Avoid catching NPE

NullPointerException (NPE) is a runtime unchecked exception and catching it is almost always a bad idea. An exception to this rule is in situations when there is no other choice and NPEs are thrown from third-party code/libraries.

Method ignores exceptional return value

When a method returns a value with special meaning, the returned value should be checked and action taken. For example, the file.delete() method deletes the files and returns a Boolean value. To verify that the file is deleted, you have to check the return value of the delete method to be true. If the deletion operation was unsuccessful, it returns false and the caller of the method should take action, probably informing the end user that the file was not deleted.

```
public boolean delete(String filename){

    File file = readFile(filename);
    boolean deleted = file.delete(); // the return value is not checked

}
```

Switch statement found where default case is missing

When writing cases for a switch statement, always provide a default case; otherwise, the logical errors may occur. For example, consider the following switch statement where according to a car's model (int value), a color is selected:

```java
public Color getCarColor(int model) {

  Color color = null;

  switch (model) {
    case 0:
      color = Color.BLACK;
      break;
    case 1:
      color = Color.BLUE;
      break;
    case 2:
      color = Color.RED;
      break;
  }

  return color;
}
```

Invoking getCarColor(1) returns BLUE but getCarColor(4) returns null because 4 is not a valid case and is a non-existent car model. In this case, the caller method has supplied an unsupported model number, and therefore this should be notified. To handle all invalid cases, we can add a default case throwing an IllegalArgumentException with an appropriate message, as shown in the following code:

```java
public Color getCarColor(int model)
  throws IllegalArgumentException{

  Color color = null;

  switch (model) {
    case 0:
      color = Color.BLACK;
      break;
    case 1:
      color = Color.BLUE;
      break;
    case 2:
```

```
        color = Color.RED;
        break;
    default:
        throw new IllegalArgumentException("Color for car model " +
model + " is undefined.");
    }

    return color;
}
```

Missing break in switch

Omitting `break` in a `switch` statement can obviously yield unexpected results. Let's visit the previous example and assume that the break for `case 0` is missing.

```
switch (model) {
    case 0:
        color = Color.BLACK; // program flow will continue to case 1
    case 1:
        color = Color.BLUE;
        break;
    case 2:
        color = Color.RED;
        break;
    default:
        throw new IllegalArgumentException("Color for car model " +
model + " is undefined.");
    }
```

Calling `getCarColor(0)` will return BLUE instead of the expected BLACK because the break statement for `case 0` is missing and code will continue execution to `case 1` until the first break.

Avoid catching Throwable

Catching `Throwable` is a bad form since it catches all kinds of exceptions—both checked and runtime ones. Runtime exceptions are supposed to be thrown at runtime and in most cases are unrecoverable, such as `OutOfMemoryError`.

The original Findbugs description of the violation explains the problem better in the following one-liner:

Catching Throwable is dangerous because it casts too wide a net.

Security rules

Finally, add eight more violations checking security issues.

Security		
Severity	Name	Analyzer
Major	HTTP Response splitting vulnerability	Findbugs
Major	HTTP cookie formed from untrusted input	Findbugs
Critical	Class exposes synchronization and semaphores in its public interface	Findbugs
Critical	Array is stored directly	PMD
Critical	Method returns internal array	PMD
Critical	Empty database password	Findbugs
Critical	A prepared statement is generated from a non-constant `String`	Findbugs
Blocker	Hardcoded constant database password	Findbugs

Class exposes synchronization and semaphores in its public interface

The Findbugs explanation on this rule is pretty clear:

A class uses synchronization along with wait(), notify() or notifyAll() on itself (the this reference). Client classes that use this class, may, in addition, use an instance of this class as a synchronizing object. Because two classes are using the same object for synchronization, Multithread correctness is suspect. You should not synchronize nor call semaphore methods on a public reference. Consider using an internal private member variable to control synchronization.

Method returns internal array

When passing arrays between objects, it is safe to always return a clone of the array and not the original one. That is because the caller can change the contents of the array affecting the array's state across all objects that reference to it. The same is applicable for lists.

If the array or list holds security-critical data then just passing it directly to a caller that can modify the reference creates a potential security risk. If you can guarantee that the caller is trusted, you can treat this violation as a false-positive.

```
public Users[] getUsers()
{
  return users;
}
```

Becomes:

```
public Users[] getUsers()
{
  return users.clone();
}
```

Hardcoded constant database password

Consider the following code where we connect using JDBC to a MySQL database:

```
public Connection createConnection() {

      try {

// load the appropriate driver
            String driverName = "com.mysql.jdbc.Driver";
            Class.forName(driverName);

// construct database url
            String serverName = "localhost";
            String database = "sonar";
            String url = "jdbc:mysql://" + serverName + "/" +
database;

// database login
            String username = "username";
            String password = "password";

            Connection connection = DriverManager.getConnection(u
rl,        username, password);

        return connection;
      }
    } catch (ClassNotFoundException ex) {
      ex1.printStackTrace();
    } catch (SQLException sqlex) {
      sqlex.printStackTrace();
    }

  }
```

Notice the database credentials in the highlighted lines are hardcoded and this triggers the violation. To resolve this, you could read the password from a properties file accessible only to the software locally.

Reading the username and password from a properties file is shown in the following code:

```
try {

// load properties file with database credentials
Properties properties = new Properties();
properties.load(new FileInputStream("database.properties"));

// load the appropriate driver
        String driverName = "com.mysql.jdbc.Driver";
        Class.forName(driverName);

// construct database url
        String serverName = "localhost";
        String database = "sonar";
        String url = "jdbc:mysql://" + serverName + "/" +
database;

// database login
        String username = properties.getProperty("username");
        String password = properties.getProperty("password");

        Connection connection = DriverManager.getConnection(u
rl,              username, password);

        return connection;
    } catch (...) {
    . . .
    }
```

The preceding code loads the `database.properties` file calling `properties.load(...)` and reads the corresponding username and password entries with `property.getProperty(...)`.

Sample properties file:

```
[database.properties]
username = sally
password = sally123
```

Installing the Violation Density plugin

The Violation Density plugin provides an alternative way to read quality for a project. Instead of getting feedback about the overall quality (Rules Compliance Index), the density plugin informs on how much the source code has violations at percentage value.

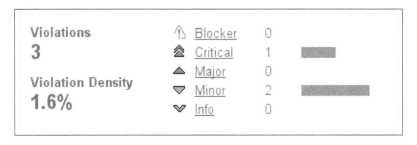

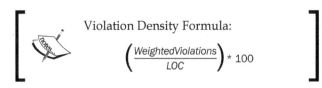

Violation Density Formula:

$$\left(\frac{WeightedViolations}{LOC}\right) * 100$$

To install the plugin, follow the same installation process for all plugins we have installed so far, remembering to restart Sonar server after installation is complete.

Integrating Sonar to Eclipse

While writing code, it is convenient to have quality and violations feedback easily available without the need to launch a web browser and review analysis results. The ideal scenario would be to have live feedback right in your IDE. This is exactly what Sonar Eclipse does, adding the Sonar perspective to your Eclipse installation. Next, we will go through the installation process of the Eclipse plugin.

Installing the Sonar Eclipse plugin

Launch Eclipse and go to **Help** and then click on **Install New Software...** from the menu.

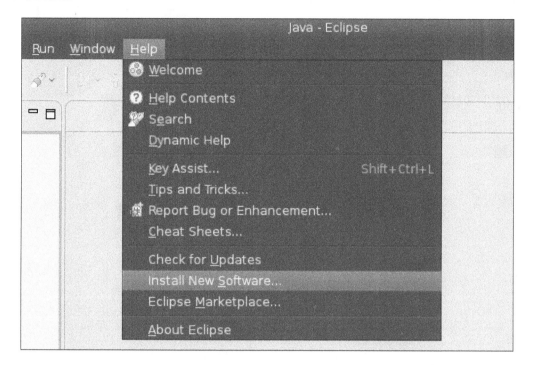

In the pop-up window, enter the URL (`http://dist.sonar-ide.codehaus.org/eclipse/`) in the **Work with** field and press *Enter* as shown in the following screenshot.

Eclipse will fetch available plugins hosted at the preceding address. Expand Sonar from the list, check **Sonar Integration for Eclipse (Required)**, and click on **Next**.

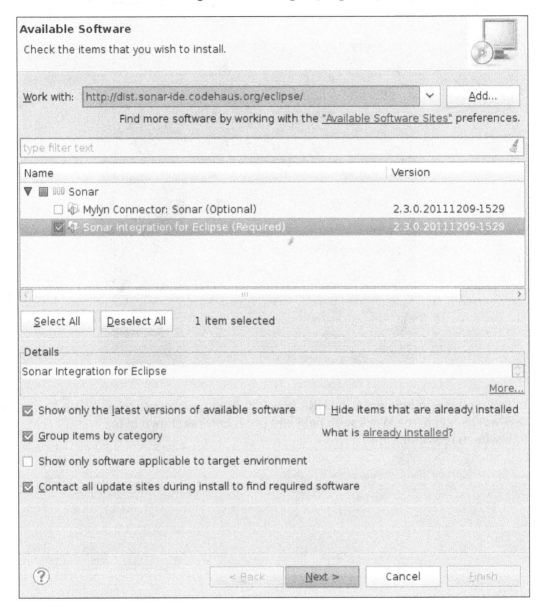

Accept the license by clicking on the appropriate radio button and click on **Next** to start the installation process.

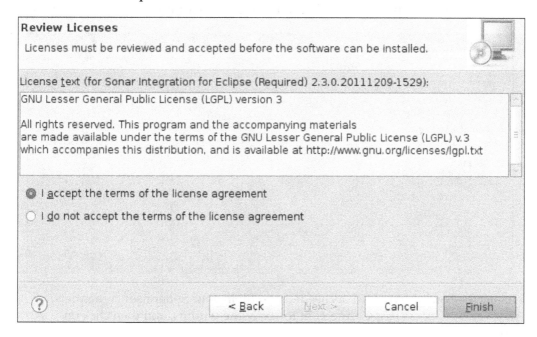

Wait for the plugin to install and restart Eclipse when prompted.

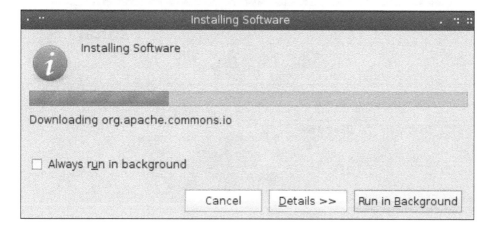

Finally, having restarted Eclipse, we have to configure the plugin. Go to **Window** from the Eclipse menu and click on **Preferences**. Find **Sonar** on the left list and click on it to view a list of preconfigured servers. Select the localhost one and click on **Edit**.

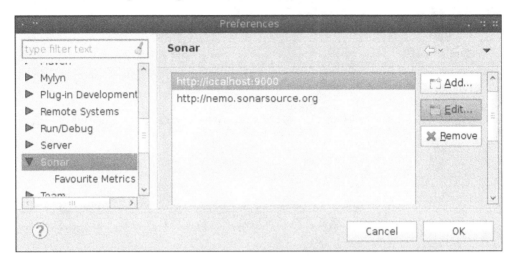

Change the Sonar server URL as needed and fill in your Sonar user credentials. Afterwards, click on **Test Connection** to verify the settings, and then click on **Finish** to save them.

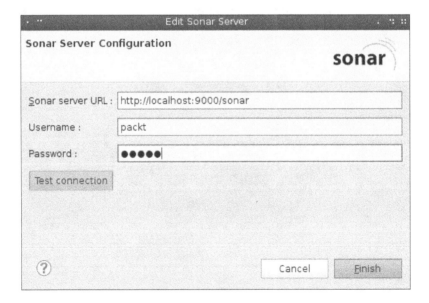

The Sonar Eclipse plugin is now fully configured and ready to use with your Eclipse projects.

Linking an Eclipse project to Sonar server

To associate a project with Sonar, right-click on a project inside the package explorer. Click on **Configure** from the pop-up menu and select **Associate with Sonar....**

Select the Sonar server where the project is hosted from the drop-down menu, select the project you want to associate to Sonar from the list, and click on **Find on Server**. The Sonar server must be running. Wait a few moments for the plugin to locate the hosted project and then click on **Finish**.

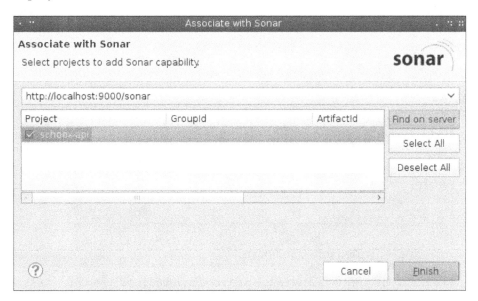

The project is now integrated with Sonar. Right-click on it in the package explorer and locate the new **Sonar** option from the menu.

From here, you can open the Sonar dashboard inside Eclipse, perform a local analysis, or disassociate the project from Sonar (**Remove Sonar Nature**).

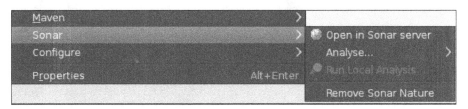

Using the Sonar perspective

To open the new Sonar perspective, go to **Window** then **Open Perspective** and select **Other** from the submenu. From the dialog that opens up, find and click on the Sonar perspective.

The Sonar perspective looks as shown in the following screenshot:

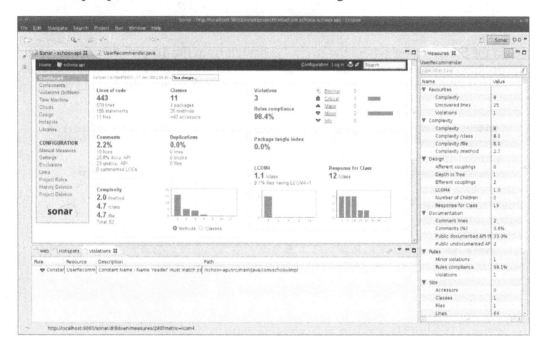

The perspective is divided into three parts:

- The central window features the project dashboard
- The right panel dynamically reads measures for any project class
- At the bottom, you can switch among three tabs: **Web**, **Hotspots**, and **Violations**

The **Measures** panel at the right gets continuously updated as you select and edit different classes inside the eclipse IDE. On the topmost place sit measures you have added to favorites for easy reference. To add a favorite measure, simply select it, right-click, and click on **Add to favorites**.

You can review violations for a class by clicking on the **Violations** tab located at the bottom panel. Double-click on a violation and the editor will focus and highlight the corresponding line in your source file. Mouse over the violation indicator on the left of the line to read a brief description about the violation. To remove a violation (a false-positive for example), right-click on it in the **Violations** tab and select **Delete** from the menu.

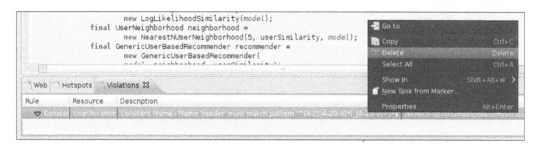

The **Hotspots** tab provides an overview about high-level metrics such as **Complexity**, **Violations**, and **Duplicated lines**. You can filter the list by selecting the desired measure. The list features classes in descending order, for example from most complex ones to simpler. Click on a class name to open it in the Java editor.

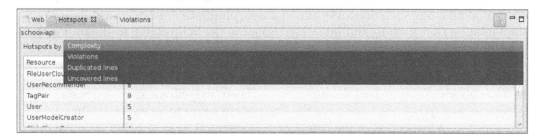

The **Web** tab hosts the Sonar Resource viewer and renders the class and all information exactly as it is seen from inside the web browser.

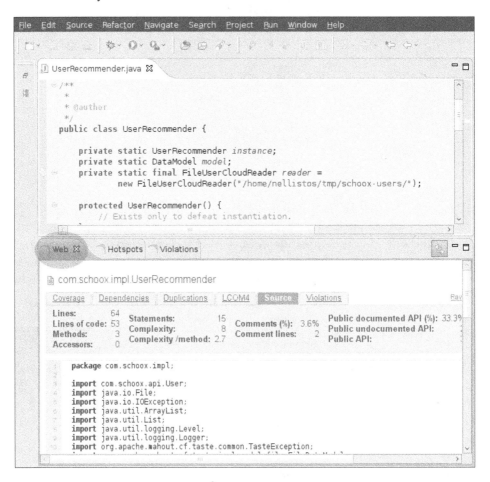

Summary

In this chapter, we saw in detail and added more Sonar rules to the *Packt profile* to cover potential bug violations. We added a new plugin to our Sonar installation, the Violation Density one, and integrated Sonar to the Eclipse IDE to streamline the development process.

In the next chapter, we will continue to work on the *Packt profile*, adding rules to cover another quality axis, documentation. Then, we will focus on the Sonar Source viewer. While we have used the component so far to locate violations, a more thorough inspection of the component is essential so as to better leverage the functionality it has to offer.

Refining Your Documentation 7

In this chapter, we will examine how we can use Sonar to evaluate results on documentation and comments levels in our projects. We will detail Sonar's metrics on documentation and comments size and add rules which govern documentation in the Packt profile. We will go through the process of locating documentation omissions using Sonar widgets and components, and finally we will configure Maven to generate documentation automatically, embedding it inside Sonar using the Sonar Doxygen plugin.

In this chapter, we cover:

- Writing effective documentation
- Documentation metrics definitions
- Overview of Sonar documentation violations
- Locating undocumented code
- Generating documentation automatically

Writing effective documentation

Undocumented code is useless code to anyone other than the developers. On the other hand, excessive documentation explaining even minor details makes code harder to read than helping the developer. All in all, the matter of writing precise and adequate documentation is outside the scope of the book, but is essential to at least provide some general pointers and references.

As you probably already know, *Javadoc* is the official documentation generation system introduced by Sun Microsystems.

How to write documentation comments for the Javadoc tool

Make sure to visit Oracle's comprehensive Javadoc guide at the following URL:

```
http://www.oracle.com/technetwork/java/javase/
documentation/index-137868.html
```

Comments structure

A Javadoc block comment starts with /** and ends with */. Lines between the opening and closing tags start with *. Single line or inline comments start with //.

Javadoc block comment

```
/**
 * Description of Method.
 * This method is responsible for...
 */
```

Javadoc line comment

```
public String foo(){
    ...
    //  TODO: return value for nulls
    return value;
}
```

Javadoc common tags

The following table lists the most commonly used Javadoc tags along with a small description:

Tag and Parameter	Usage	Applies to	Since
@author name	Describes an author.	Class, Interface, Enum	
@version version	Provides software version entry. Max one per Class or Interface.	Class, Interface, Enum	
@since since-text	Describes when this functionality first existed.	Class, Interface, Enum, Field, Method	

Tag and Parameter	Usage	Applies to	Since
`@see reference`	Provides a link to other element of documentation.	Class, Interface, Enum, Field, Method	
`@param name description`	Describes a method parameter.	Method	
`@return description`	Describes the return value.	Method	
`@exception classname description` `@throws classname description`	Describes an exception that may be thrown from this method (@exception and @throws are synonyms).	Method	
`@deprecated description`	Describes an outdated method.	Method	
`{@inheritDoc}`	Copies the description from the overridden method.	Overriding Method	1.4.0
`{@link reference}`	Link to other symbol.	Class, Interface, Enum, Field, Method	
`{@value}`	Return the value of a static field.	Static Field	1.4.0

The following is an example putting to use the previous tags:

```
/**
 * Validates a chess move.
 *
 * Use {@link #doMove(int, int, int, int)} to move a piece.
 *
 * @param theFromFile file from which a piece is being moved
 * @param theFromRank rank from which a piece is being moved
 * @param theToFile   file to which a piece is being moved
 * @param theToRank   rank to which a piece is being moved
 * @return            true if the move is valid, otherwise false
 */
boolean isValidMove(int theFromFile, int theFromRank, int theToFile,
int theToRank)
{
    ...
}

/**
 * Moves a chess piece.
 *
```

```
 * @see java.math.RoundingMode
 */
boolean doMove(int theFromFile, int theFromRank, int theToFile, int
theToRank)
{
    ...
}
```

Documentation metrics definitions

Sonar features a set of metrics to measure project documentation and comments. Before examining documentation rules, it is wise to first discuss and detail these metrics. They are available from the project dashboard within the **Comments & Duplications** widget, as shown in the following screenshot:

Comments
53.1%
22,090 lines
99.9% docu. API
1 undocu. API
38 commented LOCs

Duplications
1.7%
934 lines
65 blocks
10 files

Documentation metrics are on the left section of the widget. Click on a metric to get a list of packages/classes and their measured values.

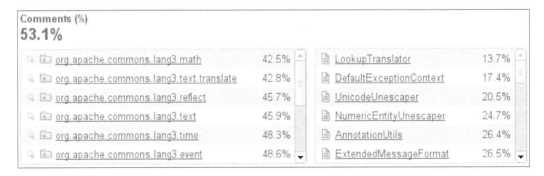

Comments (%)		
53.1%		

org.apache.commons.lang3.math	42.5%	LookupTranslator	13.7%
org.apache.commons.lang3.text.translate	42.8%	DefaultExceptionContext	17.4%
org.apache.commons.lang3.reflect	45.7%	UnicodeUnescaper	20.5%
org.apache.commons.lang3.text	45.9%	NumericEntityUnescaper	24.7%
org.apache.commons.lang3.time	48.3%	AnnotationUtils	26.4%
org.apache.commons.lang3.event	48.6%	ExtendedMessageFormat	26.5%

Metrics which measure code and documentation size are as follows:

- Physical lines: Number of carriage returns
- Comment lines: Number of comment lines
- Commented-out lines of code: Number of code lines that have been commented out

- Lines of code: Number of actual lines of code without counting blank lines, comments, commented-out code, and header file comment used for licensing

- Density of comment lines: Number of comment lines with respect to total Lines Of Code

- Public undocumented API: Number of public APIs without Javadoc documentation

- Density of public documented API: Number of public API comment lines with respect to total Lines Of Code

- Statements: Number of statements as defined in the Java Language Specification

Comment lines

Comment lines is the total number of comments inside Javadoc blocks, multi-line comments, and single-line comments.

 Empty comment lines and header comments usually used for licensing purposes are not counted.

Commented-out Lines of Code

This metric equals to the total number of commented-out lines of code. Code inside Javadoc blocks does not count towards the total. For example, the following lines are not counted because they lie inside a Javadoc block:

```
/*
 *    bar();
 *    foo();
 */
```

Density of Comment Lines

To calculate the Density of Comment Lines metric, the following formula is used:

$$DCL = \frac{commentlines}{linesofcode + commentlines} * 100$$

In the following screenshot, Sonar reports a density of **53.1%**:

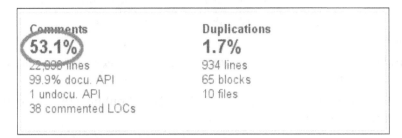

A DCL value of **50%** means that the number of lines of comments are equal to the number of lines of code. A value less than **50%** reveals that comment lines are less, while a value of **100%** means that there are only comments and no code.

Density of Public Documented API

To calculate the Density of Public Documented API (DPDA), the following formula is used:

$$DPDA = \frac{Number of PublicAPI - Number of Undocumented PublicAPI}{Number of PublicAPI} * 100$$

This is one of the most vital metrics. A project may lack in documentation but at least the public API documentation should be abundant and at high levels. That's why we are going to create an alert monitoring this measure.

Monitoring documentation levels

Next, we will use Sonar's alerting mechanism to monitor documentation on public APIs. From **Configuration** go to **Quality Profiles** and select the **packt** profile we have already created. Move on to **Alerts Tab** and create the alert as shown:

Here is how the alert shows in the project list (mouse over the icon to get more information):

Statements

This is the number of statements as defined in the Java Language Specification but without block definitions. The statements counter gets incremented by one each time an expression (if, else, while, do, for, switch, break, continue, return, throw, synchronized, catch, or finally) is encountered.

```
//
i = 0;
if (ok)
if (exit) {
if (3 == 4);
if (4 == 4) { ; }
} else {
try{}
while(true){}
for(...){}
...
```

The statements counter is not incremented by a class, method, field, annotation definition, or by a package and import declaration.

Block definitions

In Java, any sequence of statements can be grouped together to function as a single statement by enclosing the sequence in braces. These groupings are called statement blocks. A statement block may also include variable declarations. Sonar ignores such groups and counts all distinct statements within the block.

Overview of Sonar documentation violations

Sonar features a total of 10 rules that cover documentation and comments. Eight of them are of *Major* severity and two of minor. We are going to convert them all to *Major* level in order to get a rounded cost at 30 points.

Documentation and Comments Profile Distribution		
Severity	**Rules Count**	**Cost**
Major	10	30
Total Cost		30

The rules though, can be further categorized in two main categories:

- Javadoc rules
- Inline comments rules

Javadoc rules

Javadoc Rules		
Severity	**Name**	**Analyzer**
Major	Undocumented API	PMD
Major	Javadoc Method	Checkstyle
Major	Javadoc Package	Checkstyle
Major	Javadoc Style	Checkstyle
Major	Javadoc Type	Checkstyle
Major	Javadoc Variable	Checkstyle

When adding the following rules to the custom *packt* profile, change all minor severities to major:

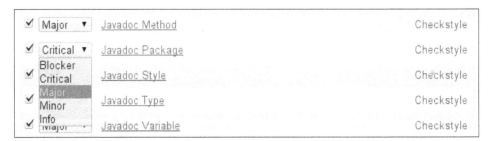

Undocumented API

Check that each public class, interface, method, and constructor has a Javadoc comment. The following public methods/constructors are not concerned by this rule:

- Getter/Setter
- Method with @Override annotation
- Empty constructor

Javadoc Method

Javadoc Method checks the Javadoc of a method or constructor. By default, it does not check for unused throws. To allow documented `java.lang.RuntimeExceptions` that are not declared, set the property `allowUndeclaredRTE` to `true`. The scope to verify is specified using the `Scope` class and defaults to `Scope.PRIVATE`. To verify another scope, set the property scope to a different scope.

Additionally, you can use the following parameters to better control the check:

Javadoc Parameter	Description
allowMissingParamTags	Suppress error messages about parameters and type parameters for which no param tags are present
allowMissingThrowsTags	Suppress error messages about exceptions which are declared to be thrown, but for which no throws tag is present
allowMissingReturnTag	Suppress error messages about methods which return non-void but for which no return tag is present

Javadoc is not required on a method that is tagged with the @Override annotation. However, under Java 5 it is not possible to mark a method required for an interface (this was corrected under Java 6). Hence, Checkstyle supports using the convention of using a single {@inheritDoc} tag instead of all the other tags.

Note that only inheritable items will allow the {@inheritDoc} tag to be used in place of comments. Static methods at all visibilities, private non-static methods, and constructors are not inheritable.

Javadoc Package

Javadoc Package checks that each Java package has a Javadoc file used for commenting. By default, it only allows the inclusion of a `package-info.java` file, but can be configured to allow `package.html` files as well. An error will be reported if both files exist, as this is not allowed by the Javadoc tool.

Javadoc Style

Javadoc Style validates Javadoc comments to help ensure they are well formed. The following checks are performed:

- Ensure the first sentence ends with proper punctuation (that is a period, question mark, or exclamation mark, by default). Javadoc automatically places the first sentence in the method summary table and index. Without proper punctuation, the Javadoc may be malformed. All items eligible for the {@inheritDoc} tag are exempt from this requirement.

- Check text for Javadoc statements that do not have any description. This includes both completely empty Javadoc, and Javadoc with only tags such as @param and @return.

- Check text for incomplete HTML tags. Verify that HTML tags have corresponding end tags and issues an Unclosed HTML tag found: error if not. An Extra HTML tag found: error is issued if an end tag is found without a previous open tag.

- Check that a package Javadoc comment is well formed (as described previously) and *not* missing from any package-info.java files.

- Check for allowed HTML tags. The allowed HTML tags are a, abbr, acronym, address, area, b, bdo, big, blockquote, br, caption, cite, code, colgroup, del, div, dfn, dl, em, fieldset, "h1" to "h6", hr, i, img, ins, kbd, li, ol, p, pre, q, samp, small, span, strong, sub, sup, table, tbody, td, tfoot, th, thread, tr, tt, and ul.

Javadoc Type

Javadoc Type checks Javadoc comments for class and interface definitions. By default, it does not check for author or version tags. The scope to verify is specified using the Scope class and defaults to Scope.PRIVATE. To verify another scope, set property scope to one of the scope constants. To define the format for an author tag or a version tag, set property authorFormat or versionFormat respectively to a regular expression.

Error messages about type parameters for which no param tags are present can be suppressed by defining property allowMissingParamTags.

Javadoc Variable

Javadoc Variable checks that a variable has Javadoc comment.

Inline Comments Rules

The following table lists the rules that check empty and uncommented constructors/methods:

Inline Comments Rules		
Severity	**Name**	**Analyzer**
Major	Uncommented Empty Constructor	PMD
Major	Uncommented Empty Method	PMD
Major	Uncommented Main	Checkstyle
Major	Comment pattern matcher	Checkstyle

Uncommented Empty Constructor

Uncommented Empty Constructor finds instances where a constructor does not contain statements, but there is no comment. By explicitly commenting empty constructors, it is easier to distinguish between intentional (commented) and unintentional empty constructors.

```
public User() {
    // Default empty constructor.
}
```

Uncommented Empty Method

Uncommented Empty Method finds instances where a method does not contain statements, but there is no comment. By explicitly commenting empty methods, it is easier to distinguish between intentional (commented) and unintentional empty methods.

```
public void init() {
    // empty initializer method.
}
```

Uncommented Main

Uncommented Main checks for uncommented `main()` methods (debugging leftovers).

Rationale: A `main()` method is often used for debugging purposes. When debugging is finished, developers often forget to remove the method, which changes the API and increases the size of the resulting class/jar file. With the exception of the real program entry points, all `main()` methods should be removed/commented out of the sources.

Locating undocumented code

The **Comments & Duplications** widget inside the project dashboard provides an overview about documentation. From there we can further browse to undocumented classes by clicking on a metric and finally getting down to source code. A typical workflow would be to:

1. Click on the **Comments** or the **Public Undocumented API** metric displayed in the widget.

2. Select a package to drill down or a class from the list.

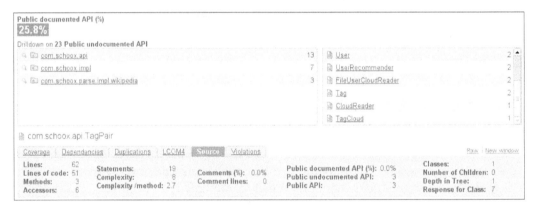

If you select a class, the source viewer opens up focused on the **Source** tab. Read on the header of the source viewer and locate the Comments metrics and the Public documented API on the third and fourth column.

3. Click on the **Violations** tab.

4. Filter the source viewer selecting Javadoc-related violations from the select menu.

Creating the documentation filter

To provide a view regarding documentation and comments for all projects, we can create a custom filter including filtered information on these topics. Log in as Administrator and from Sonar's main page click on **Add Filter** at the top left. Name it Documentation and check the **Shared** checkbox to make it available to other users. Then, click on **Save & Preview** to save the filter and move onto its configuration.

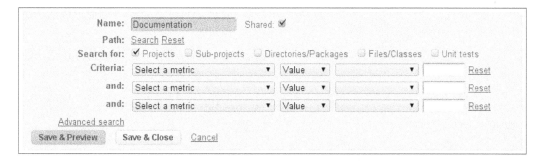

Next from the **Display** panel, we can add value columns as we desire. Select a value from the list, for example **Public documented API (%)**, and click on **Add**.

You can preview the project list at the bottom of the panel. To remove a column, click on the trashcan button and to rearrange it, click on the left/right arrow buttons.

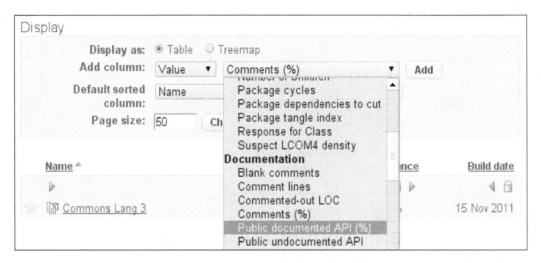

Add the documentation and comments metrics you want and click on **Save & Close** to save changes. The new filter is now available from the Sonar main page as a separate view under the **Documentation** tab. The final result should look like the following screenshot:

From now on you can use this filter to get a summary on documentation levels across all your projects.

Generating documentation automatically

Both Ant and Maven use the *Javadoc* tool to automatically generate documentation. If you are using Ant, simply navigate to a project's root directory and enter the following command:

```
$ ant javadoc
  Buildfile: build.xml


javadoc:
```

```
[javadoc] Generating Javadoc
[javadoc] Javadoc execution
[javadoc] Loading source file /home/packt/...
[javadoc] Constructing Javadoc information...
```

For Maven you first have to add the javadoc plugin. To do this, edit the pom.xml file and add the following lines at the corresponding location:

```
<project>
   ...
  <reporting>
    <plugins>
      <plugin>
        <groupId>org.apache.maven.plugins</groupId>
        <artifactId>maven-javadoc-plugin</artifactId>
        <version>2.8</version>
        <configuration>
           ...
        </configuration>
      </plugin>
    </plugins>
     ...
  </reporting>
   ...
</project>
```

From now on whenever the site goal, a$ mvn site:site, is executed, project Javadocs will be generated and included in a dedicated project site generated by Maven along with other useful project information.

Next, to provide more complete documentation featuring class diagrams, call graphs, and through class and method indexing embedded into Sonar, we will install *Graphviz* and *Doxygen*. These tools are used by the Sonar Documentation plugin to bring project documentation into the dashboard.

Installing Graphviz

Graphviz is a diagrams and networks visualization tool. It can be used to visualize program flow and produce call graphs, in an effort to complement existing documentation, and to better understand how objects interact with each other. Doxygen leverages Graphviz functionality to produce class and object interaction diagrams, including them in the final Javadoc. Visit the Graphviz official site at http://www.graphviz.org/About.php.

To install Graphviz in Linux, (Debian or Ubuntu distributions), open a terminal and enter the following command:

```
$ sudo apt-get install graphviz
```

For other Linux distributions, there are `debian` and `rpm` packages available at the Graphviz download page. Download and install the appropriate package from `http://www.graphviz.org/Download..php`.

In Windows, download the `msi` installation package from `http://www.graphviz.org/Download_windows.php` and run it.

Warning for Vista users

Even if you are logged in as Administrator, double-clicking on the MSI file or running the MSI file from a command prompt may still not provide sufficient privileges. You have to run the command `msiexec /a graphviz-x.xx.msi`.

Installing Doxygen

The Doxygen documentation system supports numerous programming languages and can generate documentation from a set of documented source files in HTML, RTF, hyperlinked PDF, and Unix man pages formats. Visit the official homepage at `http://www.stack.nl/~dimitri/doxygen/`.

If you are on Linux, you can find `rpm` and `debian` packages available at the following links:

- RPM packages: `http://www.stack.nl/~dimitri/doxygen/download.html#rpm`
- Debian packages: `http://www.stack.nl/~dimitri/doxygen/download.html#deb`

If you use the synaptic manager, you can install it by entering in the terminal the following command:

```
$ sudo apt-get install doxygen
```

For Windows, you can download the installer from `http://www.stack.nl/~dimitri/doxygen/download.html#latestsrc`.

Using the Sonar Documentation plugin

Log in to Sonar and install the Sonar Doxygen plugin from the Update Center. You need to restart the Sonar Server for the process to complete. The plugin generates documentation using Doxygen and Graphviz. The generated documentation can be browsed from the project dashboard. According to the level of drilldown inside the dashboard — project, package, or class — an appropriate documentation item is displayed, for example, list of packages, package documentation, or class documentation respectively.

To configure the plugin, go to **Configuration | General Settings**. Under **Doxygen** there are three global configuration properties as follows:

Property Name	Mandatory	Comments
Documentation Path Generation	Yes	Directory path where the documentation will be generated.
		If Sonar server is used to access the documentation, the path should be set to `/war/sonar-server`.
Web Server Deployment URL	Yes	URL to display the generated documentation.
		Sonar server can be used to access the documentation.
Directory Path	No	Directory Path containing `header.html`, `footer.html` and `doxygen.css` in order to customize HTML documentation.

Hosting Documentation

Plugin-generated documentation can be hosted within the Sonar server but this could cause performance issues. It is recommended to use an Apache server if available and change properties *Documentation Path Generation* and *Web Server Deployment URL* to `<apache.install.dir>`/www and `http://localhost:80` respectively.

From the project dashboard, click on the **Documentation** item from the left navigation menu to browse generated documentation.

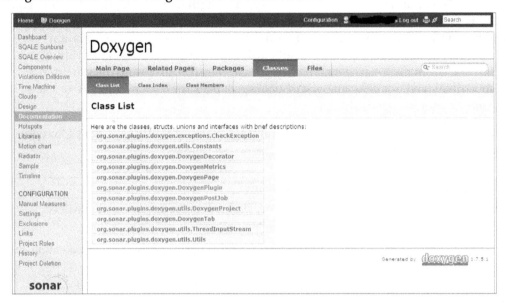

From there you can use the tabs to navigate through the documentation browsing packages, classes, and methods. If Graphviz has been installed, class call and caller graphs will be included at each page.

The plugin can be further configured at project level, by clicking **Documentation** under **Configuration** from the project dashboard. The following properties are available:

Property Name	Comments	Default
Generate Doxygen Documentation	`disable`: Do not generate documentation and delete existing documentation	`<disable>`
	`keep`: Do not generate documentation but keep previous documentation if existing	
	`enable`: Generate or regenerate documentation	
Excludes Specific Files	Comma-separated list	
Generate Class Graphs	If `true`, Graphviz must be installed	`<false>`
Generate Call Graphs	If `true`, Graphviz must be installed	`<false>`
Generate Caller Graphs	If `true`, Graphviz must be installed	`<false>`

Summary

In this chapter, we examined how Sonar manages and presents documentation levels across our projects. Having reviewed Sonar's metrics and the formulae, we added documentation and comments rules to the custom *packt* profile. We have seen how to locate documentation violations and created a custom filter to provide a summarized view on all projects regarding documentation and comments.

Finally, we installed and configured Maven's documentation plugin to automatically generate Javadoc documentation and installed the Sonar Doxygen plugin to make the project documentation available inside the project dashboard.

In the next chapter, we will learn about duplicated code and how to locate it. Sonar offers some interesting widgets to easily pin down duplicated blocks of code and lines, along with the Useless Code plugin, which aggregates duplicated source code sections and presents them across all parts inside a project. Additionally, we will see how Sonar detects duplication not only within one project but also across all of them.

8

Working with Duplicated Code

In this chapter, we will review how Sonar tracks duplication in our software application. Sonar features four essential metrics to measure duplication across projects and presents metrics in a widget format inside the project dashboard. Knowing the metrics and having created an alert when duplication metrics , we will take a look at the widget and use it to effectively drill down to our source code, locating duplicated lines and blocks. To get a top-layer view, we will use the Radiator component, as it is ideal to highlight duplication spread for large projects.

In this chapter, we will cover:

- Code duplication
- Sonar code duplication metrics
- Locating duplicated code with Sonar
- The Useless Code Tracker plugin
- Using extraction and inheritance to attack duplication

Code duplication

Duplicated code is simply copied and pasted at various places across a software project. When something "works", why not clone it and reuse by copying it? Code duplication is a sign of bad design raising complexity with no reason. What if the popular and duplicated code someday has to change or is buggy? Obviously, duplicated code would have to be corrected at numerous places across your project.

There are some common techniques such as method extraction to attack the problem, but in many cases, duplicated code highlights the inability of our design and the lack of flexibility usually requiring more advanced solutions. Of course, when resources are limited, refactoring and redesigning is a luxury. What we can do is correct the bug and yes, duplicate code if necessary and put redesign issues to the back burner. Sonar will trace duplicated blocks and remind us, and even alert us, when duplication reaches dangerous levels.

Don't Repeat Yourself (DRY)

Don't Repeat Yourself is the software development practice where code duplication is unacceptable. Similar to database systems, source code should be normalized and with every piece of code representing a single and specific functionality. This practice is better known by the DRY acronym and was introduced by Andy Hunt and Dave Thomas in their book, *The Pragmatic Programmer*.

The DRY principle:

> *Every piece of knowledge must have a single, unambiguous, authoritative representation within a system.*

Sonar code duplication metrics

Sonar uses the following four metrics to cover code duplication. Duplicated lines can also be expressed as a percentage value and we will create an alert with a threshold value of five percent.

Name	Description
Duplicated Lines	Number of physical lines touched by duplication.
Duplicated Blocks	Number of duplicated blocks participating in duplication.
Duplicated Files	Number of files containing duplicated lines or blocks.
Density of Duplicated Lines	$Density = \dfrac{DuplicatedLines}{PhysicalLines} * 100$

Creating Duplicated Code Alert

Log in to Sonar and navigate to the custom **packt** profile configuration screen. Add a new alert as shown in the following screenshot:

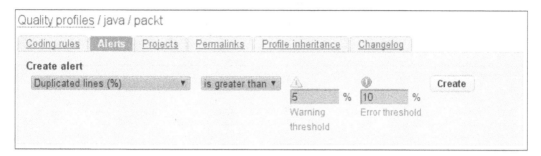

With the previous configuration, when duplication levels reach **10%** or higher, an alert at level error will be triggered. If duplication is higher than **5%**, the alert will be shown as a warning.

Locating duplicated code with Sonar

All duplication metrics are accessible from the project dashboard beside the **Comments** section. Notice how the metric in the large font is highlighted to alert us that the duplication levels are above five percent. All metrics are hyperlinks allowing us to drill down and locate the source.

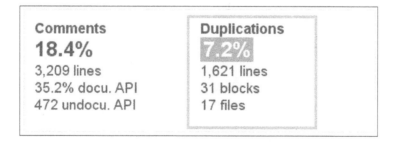

Click any of the first two metrics (percentage and number of physical lines) to navigate to the drill down screen. From left to right, you can see three panels (**Project**, **Package**, and **Class**) with the leftmost one listing all classes that contain duplicated code. The number next to a class name is the number of physical lines duplicated. Similarly, the blocks and files metrics lead to the same three-panel screen, although the numbers next to each class correspond to blocks of duplicated lines instead of raw lines.

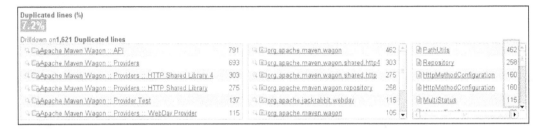

Then, click on a package to filter class results or on any class to examine it inside the source viewer. As you can see, the source viewer automatically focuses on the **Duplication** tab. The header of the tab presents the total number of lines, duplicated lines, and blocks. Below the header, you can see where actual duplication occurs at block and line level. Click on the **Expand** button to view the full block. On the left of each block, there is a list of all files which contain the duplicated code. Click on them to switch the view and examine the duplicated code in every file.

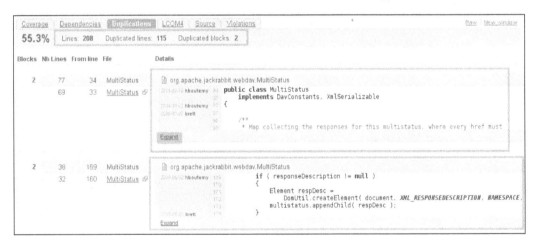

Cross-project duplication detection

Sonar also detects duplicated code across different software projects. This feedback could help us decide according to the spread of the duplication whether to export such code to an external and common library. In the following two screenshots, we see how Sonar has detected duplicated code between *Spring XML* library and a *Camel Components* library:

Method `parseInternal()` is duplicated across two different classes, `StaxStreamXmlReader` and `StaxStreamXMLReader`, an indication for a possible extension opportunity.

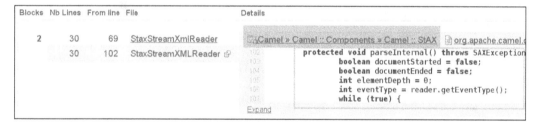

Using the Radiator component to detect duplication

The Radiator component is always useful when we want to get a top-down view on metrics, allowing us to further drill down from project to line level. So let us put it to use with duplication metrics. The component is available from any project dashboard via link in the right-hand menu.

Set the **Size** selection menu to **Duplicated lines** metric and the **Color** one to **Duplicated lines** (%). Remember that you can drill down to packages with left-click and move back up with right-click. Here is how a portion of the JDK7 looks:

Left click on the `javax.swing.plaf.multi` package to inspect how duplication is distributed among classes inside that package.

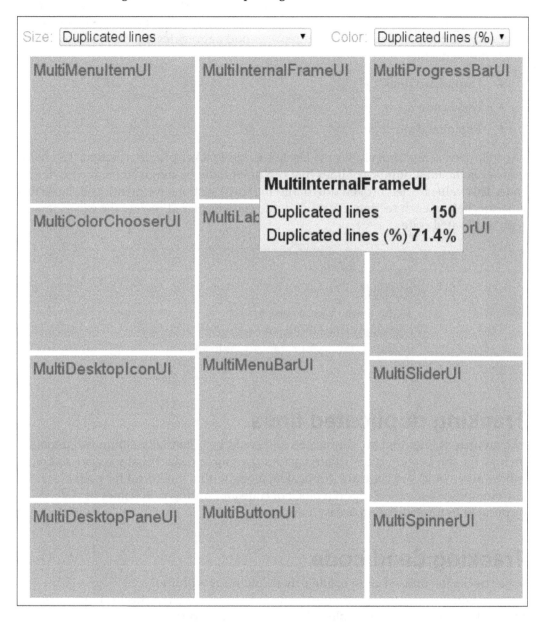

You can browse the whole JDK7 from the demo Sonar site at `http://nemo.sonarsource.org/`.

The Useless Code Tracker plugin

The Useless Code Tracker plugin is a nice addition, reporting on the total number of lines that can potentially be removed from the source code. It examines and tracks source code on the following three axes and aggregates the results into a single number value:

- Duplicated lines
- Dead code
- Potential dead code

The following screenshot shows the Useless Code Tracker plugin in action. The bold number is the total number of lines that can potentially be removed from your source code. This value is then broken down into the three sections we mentioned. Note that you can click on each section to drill down to class level and review the exact classes with duplicated code.

Useless Code

1,030

1,030 lines in duplications
0 lines in unused private methods
0 lines in unused protected methods

Tracking duplicated lines

The number of lines that are duplicated and could be potentially eliminated depends on how the duplication is distributed across the source code. What we want to know is how many blocks of code are duplicated, along with a line count for each block. For example, Sonar could report a block of code amounting to 100 lines of code duplicated in three different areas in our source code.

Tracking dead code

Sonar tracks the unused code inside private methods with the `PMD:UnusedPrivateMethod` or `SQUID:UnusedPrivateMethod` checks. Lines within these methods are eligible to be included and reported by the tracker. The same counts for unused protected methods, which are detected with the `PMD:UnusedProtectedMethod` or `SQUID:UnusedProtectedMethod` rules.

Check the configuration of the **packt** Sonar profile and make sure that the following rules are enabled:

- Squid UnusedPrivateMethod
- Squid: UnusedProtectedMethod

The Squid rules are more effective and preferred to the PMD ones because they generate less false-positives and detect more dead code.

The official description of the Squid rules concerning unused protected methods explains thoroughly when a method is considered to be *unused*.

Protected methods that are never used by any class in the same project are strongly suspected to be dead code. Dead code means unnecessary, inoperative code that should be removed. This helps in maintenance by decreasing the maintained code size, making it easier to understand the program, and preventing bugs from being introduced. Also, it could save space and compile time.

In the following cases, unused protected methods are not considered as dead code by Sonar:

- Protected methods which override a method from a parent class
- Protected methods of an abstract class

Installing the Useless Code plugin

To install the Useless Code plugin, log in to Sonar as administrator and go to **Configuration | Update Center | Available Plugins**. Find the Useless Code Tracker plugin, click on **Install**, and remember that the installation process completes after a Sonar server restart. Then, from a project dashboard, click on **Configure Widgets** at the top-left corner to bring up the widgets selection area and click on **Add** on the plugin to add it to the dashboard.

Using extraction and inheritance to attack duplication

Eliminating code duplication is not always easy, but there are some pretty straightforward refactoring techniques that help in resolving such problems. Once duplicated lines are recognized, the next step is to examine whether the duplicated code could be simply eliminated and replaced with a method call. If this is not viable, then we could resort to the *Extract Method* refactoring practice.

The Extract Method refactoring pattern

For long parts of duplicated code, we could remove the duplication by moving functionality and code to a single shared place inside our project. All parts of our program could then utilize this shared part of code instead of duplicating it.

From Martin Fowler's Refactoring book:

> *You have a code fragment that can be grouped together.*
>
> *Turn the fragment into a method whose name explains the purpose of the method.*

It is very important to provide a clear and descriptive name for the new extracted method as it is to be used from many places — wherever duplication occurs — and has to be easy to find.

Many modern IDEs support Extract Method capabilities to streamline the process. To better illustrate the process let us go through a real life example. The following code is part of a user-to-user recommendation system based on a custom user model. The highlighted code inside the `recommend()` method configures a default recommender before calling methods to perform recommendation. This chunk of code is duplicated wherever recommendation takes place, so it could be extracted to a public member method of the `UserRecommender` class.

```
public class UserRecommender {

    private static UserRecommender instance;
    private static DataModel model;
    private static final FileUserCloudReader reader;

    protected UserRecommender() {
        // Exists only to defeat instantiation.
    }

    public static UserRecommender getInstance() throws
        IOException {
```

```
        if (instance == null) {

            instance = new UserRecommender();
            final String csv = "model.csv";
            model = new FileDataModel(new File(csv));
        }

        return instance;

    }

    public List<User> recommend(
        final long id, final int max) throws IOException {

        try {

            final List<User> users = new ArrayList<User>();

          final UserSimilarity userSimilarity =
              new LogLikelihoodSimilarity(model);
          final UserNeighborhood neighborhood =
              new NearestNUserNeighborhood(5, userSimilarity,
                  model);
          final GenericUserBasedRecommender recommender =
              new GenericUserBasedRecommender(
                  model, neighborhood, userSimilarity);

            for (long userId: recommender.mostSimilarUserIDs
                (id, max)){
                users.add(reader.read(userId));
            }

            return users;

        } catch (TasteException ex) {
            Logger.getLogger(UserRecommender.class.getName()).
                    log(Level.SEVERE, null, ex);
            throw new IOException(ex.getMessage(),ex);
        }
    }

    public static DataModel getModel(){
        return model;
    }

}
```

Inside the Eclipse IDE, we select the previous highlighted code fragment and right-click to bring up the editor menu. Select **Refactor** (*Shift + Alt + T*) and **Extract Method** (*Shift + Alt + M*). We will name the extracted method as `getDefaultRecommender()`.

Clicking on the **Preview** button, we can see how our final class will be affected. Notice how the configuration lines will be replaced by a single call to the new extracted method.

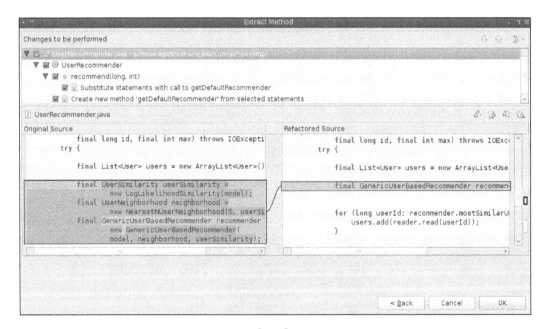

Click on **OK** to finalize the changes. Here is how the class looks like after
the extraction:

```
public class UserRecommender {

    private static UserRecommender instance;
    private static DataModel model;
    private static final FileUserCloudReader reader;

    protected UserRecommender() {
        // Exists only to defeat instantiation.
    }

    public static UserRecommender getInstance() throws
        IOException {

        if (instance == null) {

            instance = new UserRecommender();
            final String csv = "model.csv";
            model = new FileDataModel(new File(csv));
        }

        return instance;
    }

    public List<User> recommend(
            final long id, final int max) throws IOException {

        try {

            final List<User> users = new ArrayList<User>();

            final GenericUserBasedRecommender recommender =
                getDefaultRecommender();

            for (long userId: recommender.mostSimilarUserIDs
                (id, max)){
                users.add(reader.read(userId));
            }

            return users;

        } catch (TasteException ex) {
            Logger.getLogger(UserRecommender.class.getName()).
                    log(Level.SEVERE, null, ex);
            throw new IOException(ex.getMessage(),ex);
        }
    }

    public GenericUserBasedRecommender
        getDefaultRecommender()
    throws TasteException {

        final UserSimilarity userSimilarity =
            new LogLikelihoodSimilarity(model);
```

```
        final UserNeighborhood neighborhood =
            new NearestNUserNeighborhood
                (5, userSimilarity, model);
        final GenericUserBasedRecommender recommender =
            new GenericUserBasedRecommender(
            model, neighborhood, userSimilarity);

        return recommender;
    }

    public static DataModel getModel(){
        return model;
    }

}
```

Refactoring with inheritance

In another very simple example, let's suppose that we want to create a new user recommender that configures or acts a little differently. Instead of copying and pasting the existing one and duplicating code, we inherit the functionality by subclassing.

The class UserCorrelation extends UserRecommender and changes the similarity model in the following highlighted lines of code. All other methods and members remain the same.

```
public class UserCorrelation extends UserRecommender {

    public GenericUserBasedRecommender getDefaultReccommender()
            throws TasteException {

        final UserSimilarity userSimilarity =
          new PearsonCorrelationSimilarity(getModel());
        final UserNeighborhood neighborhood =
            new NearestNUserNeighborhood
                (2, userSimilarity, getModel());
        final GenericUserBasedRecommender recommender =
            new GenericUserBasedRecommender(
                getModel(), neighborhood, userSimilarity);
        return recommender;
    }

}
```

Summary

In this chapter, we saw what metrics Sonar uses to track code duplication and how to use the code widget inside the project dashboard to locate duplicated code. Sonar covers duplication not only at line block and file level in a single project but detects duplicate code across separate projects too. We created an alert to notify us when duplication reaches threshold values and used the Radiator component to get a better synopsis on duplication and its spread.

Finally, we briefly discussed two of the most common techniques in an effort to attack duplication problems such as method extraction and inheritance.

In the next chapter, we will discuss complexity and review some of the more advanced and critical metrics Sonar features.

9
Analyzing Complexity and Design

In this chapter, we will discuss how Sonar reports on complexity and the measures it supports. Firstly, we will clarify how complexity in Java programs is calculated and then look into the concepts of coupling, cohesion, and dependencies.

Finally, we will review how Sonar reports on those measures and especially detail the design matrix, which is an essential component to manage dependencies in complex software pieces.

In this chapter we will cover:

- Measuring software complexity
- Cohesion and coupling
- Sonar code complexity metrics
- The Response for Class metric
- Lack of cohesion and the LCOM4 metric
- Locating and eliminating dependencies

Measuring software complexity

Software and its complexity could be described as of how difficult it is to understand, alter, or extend the internal interaction of its components. The more complex the components of the software are, the more difficult it is to change them or add new functionality and features, preserving stability. In some cases, large complexity can even negate refactoring techniques because of the great effort required. A quicker solution would be to totally rewrite those complex pieces of code.

There are many different metrics to measure the complexity of a software component. Cyclomatic Complexity evaluates the complexity of methods in isolation, while Response for Class, Coupling, and Cohesion examine the complexity of the component in correlation to other interacting components.

The Cyclomatic Complexity metric

Cyclomatic Complexity was introduced by Thomas J. McCabe, and is the most popular and widely accepted method of measuring code complexity. The metric defines a formula to calculate the complexity of code by taking into account all the possible independent paths that program flow could follow. For instance, code with multiple decision points (if - else) and loops will rank as more complex than raw statements.

The execution path of a method could be laid out as a graph flow with nodes representing statements, decision points, loops, and exit points. Edges connect the nodes according to the code. To make this clear, let's look at following simple method, which checks whether a number is prime or not. The method consists of a few statements, a `while` loop, an `if` decision, and a `return` exit point:

```
public static boolean isPrime(int n) {
    boolean prime = true;
    int i = 2;
    while (i < n) {
        if (n % i == 0) {
        prime = false;
    }
    i++;
    }
    return prime;
}
```

To produce the graph, let's assign a node to each statement with letters from A to G, to a total of seven nodes (**N = 7**).

Node	Code
	`public static boolean isPrime(int n) {`
A	`boolean prime = true;`
B	`int i = 2;`
C	`while (i < n) {`
D	`if (n % i == 0) {`
E	`prime = false;`
	`}`

Node	Code
F	i++;
	}
G	return prime;
}	

A graph representation for the given method would look like the one shown in the following diagram. Following the statements of the code, we connect the nodes with edges. For multiple outcomes (for example, an `if` condition), we connect all possible nodes for each outcome. For example, from node C we could proceed to D in case `i < n`. But if `i >= n` execution flow would skip the `while` block and continue to node G, this is represented in the graph by connecting node C to both D and G.

The total number of connections or edges equals to 8 (**E = 8**).

Finally, the number of exit points equals to 1 for the single `return` call at the end of the method (**P = 1**).

To calculate the Cyclomatic Complexity for this method, use the following formula:

M = E − N + 2*P = 8 − 7 + 2*1 = 3.

Hence, the Cyclomatic Complexity for the `isPrime(..)` method equals to 3 (**CC = 3**).

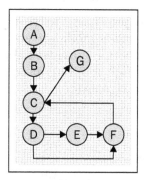

In general, when calculating Cyclomatic Complexity in Java, add one point of CC each time you encounter one of the following:

Type	Add one CC whenever you encounter:
Methods	return
Control flow	if, else, case, default
Loops	for, do, while, break, continue

Type	Add one CC whenever you encounter:
Operators	`&&, ||, ?, :, ^, &, |`
Exception handling	`catch, throw, throws, finally`
Threads	`start()`

For example, we can quickly calculate that the following method has CC of 3:

```
public int getValue(int param1) {

    int value = 0;
    if (param1 == 0)  {  (+1)
      value = 4;
    } else {  (+1)
      value = 0;
    }
    return value;  (+1)


}
```

Cohesion and coupling

In **object-oriented programming (OOP)**, cohesion and coupling are two fundamental concepts. The basic principle is to have classes with loose coupling and high cohesion. Loose coupling enables modularized packages that do not heavily rely on each other, while high cohesion provides tight and solid components with clearly defined responsibilities. **High coupling** means that a class relies on many other classes, while low cohesion signals for a class could be split into separate ones, offering fine-grained functionality.

Afferent coupling

Afferent (incoming) coupling is the total number of classes that depend on a given class. In Sonar, you can view afferent coupling within the Sonar source viewer under the **Dependencies** tab. For example, the afferent coupling for the class `ReflectionToStringBuilder` in the Apache `commons-lang` project equals to **4**. Type the class name in the top-right search box from Sonar to find the class and open it in the source viewer. Then, click on the **Dependencies** tab to view the list of classes that import `ReflectionToStringBuilder`:

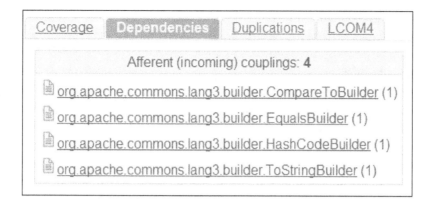

Efferent coupling

On the contrary, **efferent (outgoing) coupling** is the number of classes on which a given class depends, and has to be imported. For `ReflectionToStringBuilder`, the efferent coupling equals to **3** as you can see in the **Dependencies** tab:

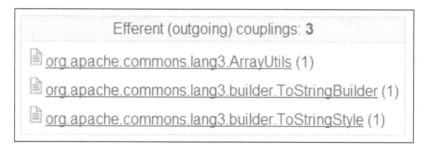

Sonar Code Complexity metrics

Sonar hosts a wide selection of complexity-related rules to help us monitor our software projects. Next, we are going to add 17 rules of major severity to the custom `packt` profile.

Complexity rules profile distribution		
Severity	**Rules count**	**Value**
Major	17	17 x 3 = 51
Total value		**51**

Log in to Sonar as administrator and add the following rules to the custom `packt` profile:

Complexity rules		
Severity	**Name**	**Analyzer**
Major	Boolean Expression Complexity	Checkstyle
Major	Class Data Abstraction coupling	Checkstyle
Major	Class Fan Out Complexity	Checkstyle
Major	Cyclomatic Complexity	Checkstyle
Major	JavaNCSS	Checkstyle
Major	Nested For Depth	Checkstyle
Major	Nested If Depth	Checkstyle
Major	Nested Try Depth	Checkstyle
Major	Simplify Boolean Expression	Checkstyle
Major	Simplify Boolean Return	Checkstyle
Major	Too many fields	PMD
Major	Too many methods	PMD
Major	Avoid too complex class	Sonar
Major	Avoid too complex method	Sonar
Major	Avoid too deep inheritance tree	Sonar
Major	Avoid using 'break' branching statement outside a 'switch' statement	Sonar
Major	Avoid using 'continue' branching statement	Sonar

Boolean Expression Complexity

This rule restricts the total number of Boolean operators within an expression. The default value is three, but can be overridden from the profile configuration screen. Whenever an expression with more operators is parsed, a violation will be thrown. The operators checked are ||, &&, |, &, and ^.

For example the following expression will raise a violation:

```
if ( ( a == b && c == d ) || ( e ==f && e==g) || a == g ){
    ...
}
```

Too many conditions render code difficult to read and debug. Additionally, the effort to unit test multiple conditions and achieve high-test coverage grows exponentially.

Class Data Abstraction Coupling

Data Abstraction Coupling (DAC) measures the number of instantiations of other classes within the given class — it is not caused by inheritance. If a class has a local variable that is an instantiation (object) of another class, there is data abstraction coupling. A DAC higher than 7 indicates an overly complicated class structure.

The maximum threshold allowed is 7 and can be configured to your liking from Sonar profile configuration screen.

Class Fan Out Complexity

Class Fan Out Complexity (CFOC) measures the number of classes on which the given class depends. A class with high CFOC has high responsibility featuring many imported classes and high efferent coupling.

The default checkstyle threshold is 20. A value higher than this indicates a complex class that could be refactored into separate components.

Cyclomatic Complexity

Checkstyle's default value for Cyclomatic Complexity is 10. Methods which report higher values will trigger a violation.

JavaNCSS

JavaNCSS determines the complexity of methods, classes, and files by counting the **Non Commenting Source Statements (NCSS)**. This check adheres to the specification for the JavaNCSS-Tool written by Chr. Clemens Lee. Roughly said, the NCSS metric is calculated by counting the source lines that are not comments and it is (nearly) equivalent to counting the semicolons and opening curly braces. The NCSS for a class is summarized from the NCSS of all its methods, the NCSS of its nested classes, and the number of member variable declarations. The NCSS for a file is summarized from the NCSS of all its top-level classes, the number of imports, and the package declaration.

Too large methods and classes are hard to read and costly to maintain. A large NCSS number often means that a method or class has too many responsibilities and/or functionalities, which should be decomposed into smaller units.

Nested For Depth

This rule restricts nested `for` blocks to a specified depth – the default value is 1. A loop within a loop will trigger a violation.

Simplify Boolean Return

This checks for overly complicated Boolean `return` statements. For example, consider the following code:

```
if (valid())
    return false;
else
    return true;
```

This could be written as:

```
return !valid();
```

Too many methods

A class with too many methods is probably a good suspect for refactoring, in order to reduce its complexity and find a way to have more fine-grained objects.

Too many fields

Classes that have too many fields could be redesigned to have fewer fields, possibly through some nested object grouping of some of the information. For example, a class with `city`, `state`, or `zip` fields could instead have one `Address` field.

Avoid too complex class

This check is similar to Checkstyle's Cyclomatic Complexity, but it is implemented by the Squid rule engine. The default maximum complexity value per class is 200.

Avoid too deep inheritance tree

Inheritance is certainly one of the most valuable concepts of object-oriented programming. It is a way to compartmentalize and re-use code by creating collections of attributes and behaviors called **classes**, which can be based on previously created classes. However, abusing this concept by creating a deep inheritance tree can lead to very complex and unmaintainable source code.

Most of the time, a too deep inheritance tree is due to bad object-oriented design, which has led to systematic use of inheritance when composition would suit better.

To view the level of inheritance for a class, open it from Sonar and look at the header for the **Depth in Tree** value:

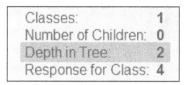

The Response for Class metric

The **Response for Class (RFC)** metric is the total number of methods that can potentially be executed in response to a message received by an object of a class. This number is the sum of the methods of the class, and all distinct methods are invoked directly within the class methods. Additionally, inherited methods are counted, but overridden methods are not, because only one method of a particular signature will always be available to an object of a given class.

> The **Response Set (RS)** of a class is a set of methods that can potentially be executed by an object of that class. RFC is the count of these methods belonging to the set.

Notice that a given method is counted only once even if it is invoked many times in the call graph as a response to a message. Classes with high RFC are more complex and prove to be difficult to debug and test, because of high cross-object communication and higher variance in the potential responses and call graphs, as responses to messages received by that class.

In Sonar, you can get information for the RFC metric from the project dashboard. The following screenshot shows the average RFC for the Apache `commons-lang` project. Below the **Response for Class** value, there is a distribution graph showing the RFC value per class count in steps of five. From the graph, you can identify that most classes fall in the 5 to 20 RFC area and that there are less than five classes with RFC of 90 to 95. A healthy distribution is to have substantially more classes with low RFC, and less as the RFC metric increases.

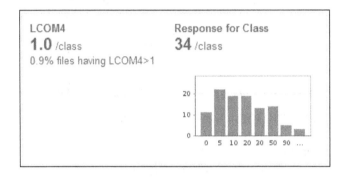

Click on the RFC metric value from the project dashboard to browse to a two-panel screen listing packages on the left, and their respective classes on the right. The number beside each class is the RFC for that class. The number inside the packages panel is the average RFC for the classes of that package. Clicking in any package will filter the classes' panel, while clicking on a class name will open up the class below the panel, within the Sonar source browser.

Find and click on the **org.apache.commons.lang3.text.translate** package from the left panel, and then click on the **AggregateTranslator** class from the right:

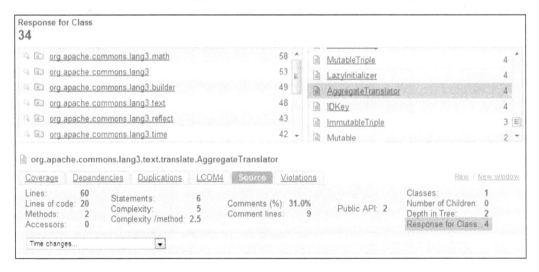

To better understand how the RFC is calculated, let's examine the simple `AggregateTranslator` class. The source code for the class is presented below with header licensing details omitted for clarity. The RFC value for `AggregateTranslator` equals to 4.

The class featured one constructor `AggregateTranslator(...)` (+1) and one method `int translate(...)` (+1). This brings RFC to a total of 2. The highlighted parts of the following code show the additional method calls that contribute to RFC also.

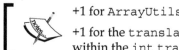
- +1 for `ArrayUtils.clone(...)` within the constructor
- +1 for the `translator.translate(...)` method within the `int translate(...)` method

These additional calls bring the total RFC value to 4.

```
package org.apache.commons.lang3.text.translate;

import java.io.IOException;
import java.io.Writer;

import org.apache.commons.lang3.ArrayUtils;

/**
 * Executes a sequence of translators one after the other. Execution
   ends whenever
 * the first translator consumes codepoints from the input.
 *
 * @since 3.0
 * @version $Id: AggregateTranslator.java 1088899 2011-04-05 05:31:27Z
   bayard $
 */
public class AggregateTranslator extends CharSequenceTranslator {

    private final CharSequenceTranslator[] translators;

    /**
     * Specify the translators to be used at creation time.
     *
     * @param translators CharSequenceTranslator array to aggregate
     */
    public AggregateTranslator(CharSequenceTranslator... translators)
{
        this.translators = ArrayUtils.clone(translators);
    }

    /**
```

```
 *   The first translator to consume codepoints from the input is
     the 'winner'.
 *   Execution stops with the number of consumed codepoints being
     returned.
 *   {@inheritDoc}
 */
@Override
public int translate(CharSequence input, int index, Writer out)
throws IOException {
    for (CharSequenceTranslator translator : translators) {
        int consumed = translator.translate(input, index, out);
        if(consumed != 0) {
            return consumed;
        }
    }
    return 0;
}
```

The AggregateTranslator class extends the CharSequenceTranslator which has an RFC of 20. Why does AggregateTranslator end up with an RFC of only 4?

This is because Sonar does not take into account the parent class when calculating RFC.

Lack of Cohesion in Methods and the LCOM4 metric

The **Lack of Cohesion in Methods (LCOM)** metric measures the cohesion of a class and it was first introduced in the Chidamber & Kemerer metrics suite in 1993. Since then, the metric was redefined and revised numerous times, with LCOM5 being the latest version.

Sonar incorporates version four of the metric, hence the LCOM4 naming. The metric measures the degree to which methods and fields within a class are related to one another, providing one or more components. To calculate the LCOM4 value, we have to determine how many connected groups of related methods and fields exist in a class:

- LCOM4 = 1: The class is a solid component with all methods and fields related
- LCOM4 > 1: The class can be split to different classes
- LCOM4 = 0: The class has no methods

According to the single responsibility principle, a class should provide a single component with all methods and fields related. This is the case when LCOM4 = 1. Otherwise, the class lacks cohesion and could be broken down to separate less complex classes with single responsibilities.

To better understand how LCOM4 is calculated, consider a class consisting of methods A, B, C, and D and fields x,y, and z. A method that invokes another class method or accesses a field is considered connected to that method or field and vice versa.

In the first example, method A invokes method B, which accesses field x, and method C invokes method D, which accesses fields y and z:

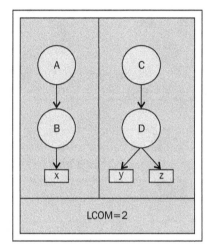

As shown in the preceding diagram, the class contains two separate components and could potentially be split into two different classes, one with methods A and B and field x, and the other with methods C and D and fields x and z.

If method C invokes method A or B or accesses field x, the result is one connected component and the class has an LCOM4 equal to 1:

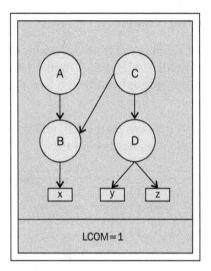

Sonar reports LCOM4 from the project dashboard along with a distribution graph similar to the one for the RFC metric. The first value is the average LCOM4 per class and the second is the total percentage of classes that have an LCOM4 higher than 1; hence they lack cohesion. Click on any of the two values to navigate to the two-panel view with packages on the left and classes on the right.

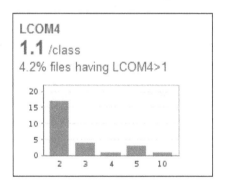

Click on a class to open up the Sonar source browser with focus on the **LCOM4** tab, as shown in the following screenshot. Sonar will present the identified separately connected components within the class in panels. Each block contains the related methods and fields for that group—yellow circles mark the fields, and red circles mark the methods.

Coverage	Dependencies	Duplications	LCOM4	Source	Violations

Lack of Cohesion of Methods: **2**

1
   ⓘ children
   ⓘ nChildren
   ⓜ addChild(ILorg/apache/maven/repository/metadata/MetadataTreeNode;)V

2
   ⓘ md
   ⓘ parent
   ⓜ graphHash()Ljava/lang/String;

Exceptions to the LCOM4 metric

So far, the LCOM4 metric identifies broad classes that can be broken into smaller and lighter ones. However, there are cases and practices where a high LCOM4 value is natural, for example, classes with the responsibility to instantiate and configure other objects such as Factories. The same stands for data structures—simple JavaBeans classes that act as field containers—or utility classes that host static helper methods. Sonar will report an expected high LCOM4 value.

At the time of writing, Sonar does not support marking such reporting as false-positives, but there is an open ticket at Sonar's issue tracking system labeled **No rule "LCOM4 is too high"** at `http://jira.codehaus.org/browse/SONAR-2686` and this will be implemented in a future version of Sonar.

According to the ticket, Sonar will introduce a new configurable LCOM4 rule. We will be able to configure a low LCOM4 threshold value and a new violation will be triggered whenever a class's LCOM4 exceeds this value. In the case of a false-positive, we will be able to review the violation and define it as a false-positive from within the Sonar source viewer.

Locating and eliminating dependencies

Sonar provides a widget to report on package and class dependencies. The following screenshot shows what Sonar reports on the `commons-lang` project. This is the entry point when you want to review highly coupled classes and locate dependencies that deteriorate the modularization of your packages.

Click on any number to navigate to Sonar's design matrix view. Alternatively, you can click on the **Design** link from the left menu.

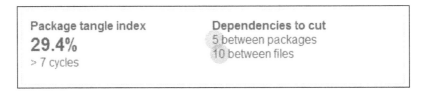

Sonar reports 5 dependencies between packages and 10 between files. The design matrix lists all project packages on the left,. The right-hand side section is separated into two triangular regions. You will notice that all dependencies to be cut are located within the upper-right triangle. The circled area encloses all 5 package dependencies and the sum of the numbers equals to 10, which is the dependency between files. In Java, this means that there are ten imports spread in classes within five packages that should be cut in order to preserve package modularization.

Packages at the bottom should not be depending on packages that reside above them at a higher level. They should exist as standalone packages to enable modularization and improve reusability.

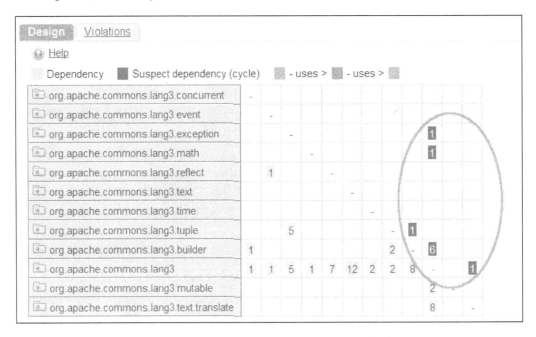

Click on any number within the triangles to open a new panel below the matrix, further detailing the dependencies. For example, clicking on number **6** reveals the following dependencies:

Dependent Package	Source Package
`org.apache.commons.lang3.AnnotationUtils`	`org.apache.commons.lang3.builder.ToStringBuilder`
`org.apache.commons.lang3.AnnotationUtils`	`org.apache.commons.lang3.builder.ToStringStyle`
`org.apache.commons.lang3.ArrayUtils`	`org.apache.commons.lang3.builder.EqualsBuilder`
`org.apache.commons.lang3.ArrayUtils`	`org.apache.commons.lang3.builder.HashCodeBuilder`
`org.apache.commons.lang3.ArrayUtils`	`org.apache.commons.lang3.builder.ToStringBuilder`
`org.apache.commons.lang3.ArrayUtils`	`org.apache.commons.lang3.builder.ToStringStyle`

Using the Sonar design matrix

Next, we will focus on the functionality of the Sonar design matrix. It is essential to understand how it works in order to efficiently identify and understand a project's dependencies.

From the left column, click on the package named **org.apache.commons.lang**. Now, the triangular region of the matrix is highlighted to denote this package's dependencies. Package rows above the selected one will be highlighted on their tip with a striped box if they depend on it—the legend on the top of the matrix explains the different highlights. In this case, we see that all packages above `lang3` are striped and hence they are dependent. To find how many files depend on `lang3`, cross reference the packages with the numbers in the horizontal highlighted row.

In the following screen, two of the total nine dependent packages are marked with lines to their respective number in the horizontal row:

- **org.apache.commons.lang3.event** has **1** file dependency
- **org.apache.commons.lang3.tuple** has **2** file dependencies

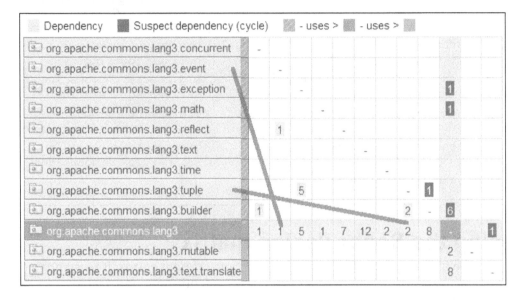

The following table lists all packages dependent on `org.apache.commons.lang3` and shows the number of their file dependencies.

Package name	Total dependencies
org.apache.commons.lang3.concurrent	1
org.apache.commons.lang3.event	1
org.apache.commons.lang3.exception	5
org.apache.commons.lang3.math	1
org.apache.commons.lang3.reflect	7
org.apache.commons.lang3.text	12
org.apache.commons.lang3.time	2
org.apache.commons.lang3.tuple	2
org.apache.commons.lang3.builder	8

Packages on which our selected `lang3` depends have their rows highlighted on their tip with a solid square—not striped. These rows are located below our selected package. The matrix shows that package **org.apache.commons.lang3** depends on `*.mutable` and `*.translate`. The number of the file dependencies equals to the corresponding box within the vertical highlighted row:

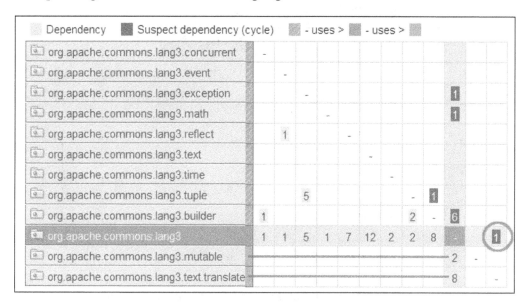

The following table lists all packages on which `org.apache.commons.lang3` depends and shows the number of their file dependencies:

Package name	Total dependencies
org.apache.commons.lang3.mutable	2
org.apache.commons.lang3.text.translate	8

So far, we have seen how to read package dependencies by using the design matrix. To view class dependencies, you can click on any number within the triangular region to open a panel listing class dependencies for the corresponding package. For example, click on the lower-right box numbered **8**. Notice that the box **8** and and its upper diagonal box numbered **1** have different color shades and are the points where the two highlighted lines cross (striped line and solid line intersect).

The number **8** means that package **org.apache.commons.lang3** has eight dependencies on package **org.apache.commons.lang3.text.translate** (remember that striped boxes depend on solid ones). The number **1** in the upper triangular region alerts us to a cross dependency back to package `*.lang3` which is eligible for elimination. You can click on all numbers in the upper triangular region to further inspect potential cross dependencies:

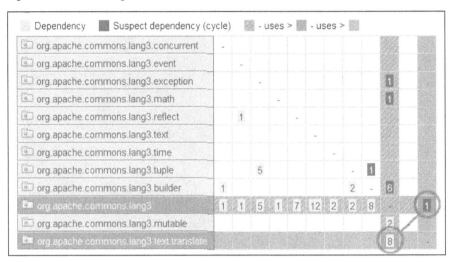

The following table lists all class dependencies from the package `org.apache.commons.lang3` to `org.apache.commons.lang3.text.translate`:

Dependent Package	Source Package
org.apache.commons.lang3.StringEscapeUtils	org.apache.commons.lang3.text.translate.AggregateTranslator
org.apache.commons.lang3.StringEscapeUtils	org.apache.commons.lang3.text.translate.CharSequenceTranslator
org.apache.commons.lang3.StringEscapeUtils	org.apache.commons.lang3.text.translate.EntityArrays
org.apache.commons.lang3.StringEscapeUtils	org.apache.commons.lang3.text.translate.LookupTranslator
org.apache.commons.lang3.StringEscapeUtils	org.apache.commons.lang3.text.translate.NumericEntityUnescaper
org.apache.commons.lang3.StringEscapeUtils	org.apache.commons.lang3.text.translate.OctalUnescaper
org.apache.commons.lang3.StringEscapeUtils	org.apache.commons.lang3.text.translate.UnicodeEscaper
org.apache.commons.lang3.StringEscapeUtils	org.apache.commons.lang3.text.translate.UnicodeUnescaper

To better understand the process, we will pinpoint one dependency at line level. To do so, click on the box numbered **1** as shown in the following screenshot, and then click on the **org.apache.commons.lang3.text.translate.AggregateTranslator** class to open it in the Sonar source viewer.

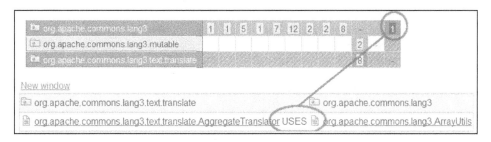

As you can see from the highlighted parts in the following code, the translator imports `ArrayUtils` to clone an array of translators in the method `translate(...)`:

```
package org.apache.commons.lang3.text.translate;

import java.io.IOException;
import java.io.Writer;

import org.apache.commons.lang3.ArrayUtils;

/**
 * Executes a sequence of translators one after the other. Execution
   ends whenever
 * the first translator consumes codepoints from the input.
 *
 * @since 3.0
 * @version $Id: AggregateTranslator.java 1088899 2011-04-05 05:31:27Z
   bayard $
 */
public class AggregateTranslator extends CharSequenceTranslator {

    private final CharSequenceTranslator[] translators;

    /**
     * Specify the translators to be used at creation time.
     *
     * @param translators CharSequenceTranslator array to aggregate
     */
    public AggregateTranslator(CharSequenceTranslator... translators)
{
```

```
        this.translators = ArrayUtils.clone(translators);
    }


    /**
     * The first translator to consume codepoints from the input is
       the 'winner'.
     * Execution stops with the number of consumed codepoints being
       returned.
     * {@inheritDoc}
     */
    @Override
    public int translate(CharSequence input, int index, Writer out)
    throws IOException {
        for (CharSequenceTranslator translator : translators) {
            int consumed = translator.translate(input, index, out);
            if(consumed != 0) {
                return consumed;
            }
        }
        return 0;
    }


}
```

As the dependency is not widespread and if you want to move the `*.lang3.text.translate` package to another library or make it standalone, you can implement the `ArrayUtils.clone` method within `AggregateTranslator` as a private method and lose the dependency, especially, when it is only a few lines of code:

```
private <T> T[] clone(T[] array) {
        if (array == null) {
            return null;
        }
        return array.clone();
    }
```

Next, double-click on the **org.apache.commons.lang3.text.translate** package row from the left-hand side of the matrix to drill down to class level. The design matrix represents dependencies in the same manner, but only for the classes within the selected package.

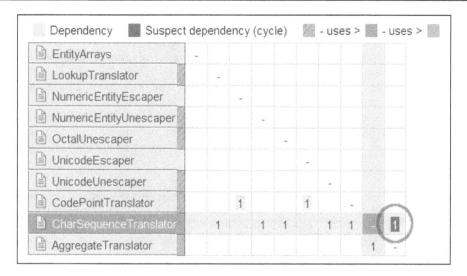

As you can see, `CharSequenceTranslator` has an illegal dependency
on `AggregateTrnalstor`. To investigate further, double-click on
CharSequenceTranslator to view its source code—highlighted code shows that a
new instance of `AggregateTranslator` is returned from the `translate` method.
As you can see, `CharSequenceTranslator` is an abstract class, which is extended
by `AggregateTranslator`. It is quite restrictive to use an instance of a child class
within the abstract. Additionally, the responsibility to use aggregated translation
methods from many translators can be moved in the abstract class or exclusively
in the `AggregateTranslator`:

```
package org.apache.commons.lang3.text.translate;

import java.io.IOException;
import java.io.StringWriter;
import java.io.Writer;
import java.util.Locale;

/**
 * An API for translating text.
 * Its core use is to escape and unescape text. Because escaping and
   unescaping
 * is completely contextual, the API does not present two separate
   signatures.
 *
 * @since 3.0
 * @version $Id: CharSequenceTranslator.java 1146844 2011-07-14
   18:49:51Z mbenson $
 */
public abstract class CharSequenceTranslator {
```

```
...

/**
 * Helper method to create a merger of this translator with
   another set of
 * translators. Useful in customizing the standard functionality.
 *
 * @param translators CharSequenceTranslator array of translators
   to merge with this one
 * @return CharSequenceTranslator merging this translator with the
   others
 */
public final CharSequenceTranslator with(CharSequenceTranslator...
translators) {
    CharSequenceTranslator[] newArray = new CharSequenceTranslator
    [translators.length + 1];
    newArray[0] = this;
    System.arraycopy(translators, 0, newArray, 1, translators.
    length);
    return new AggregateTranslator(newArray);
}

...

}
```

Ideally, when all dependencies are resolved the design matrix would have an empty upper triangle, with all dependencies sitting in the lower one. Moreover, packages at lower levels tend to be more used and imported from packages at higher levels. So, the lower rows of the triangle would naturally be more populated with numbers denoting dependencies on upper packages.

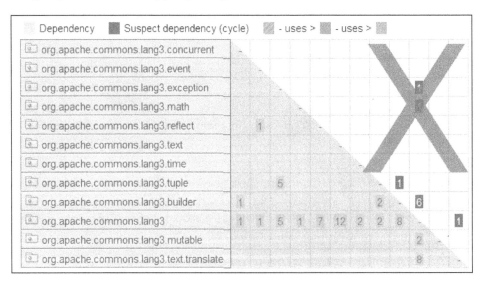

Summary

In this chapter, we discussed software complexity. We also discussed how it is measured and what Sonar can offer in order to help us identify complex constructs. We saw some core measures and metrics that govern complexity such as Cyclomatic Complexity, Coupling and Cohesion, Response for Class, and Lack of Cohesion. Then, we added the appropriate rules to the Sonar profile and examined all widgets reporting such measures. At the end of the chapter, we focused on dependencies and detailed the Sonar design matrix, an invaluable component, which, once mastered, will enable you to isolate dependencies in a quick and efficient way.

In the next chapter, we will discuss how Sonar measures Test Coverage and Testing, as it is an essential and vital practice towards quality software. Testing and coverage is the countermeasure towards complex software ensuring stability and expected behavior.

10
Code Coverage and Testing

In this chapter, we will discuss how Sonar analyzes our unit tests, evaluating different code coverage criteria. The goal is to have Sonar identify untested code and guide developers as to what tests need to be written to improve the software quality. The platform leverages the functionality of popular Java code coverage engines and analyzes the collected coverage data taking into account other software measures such as complexity. Thus, Sonar enhances the monolithic code coverage analysis, as it adds more layers of information on top of percentile coverage results.

For example, low-complexity statements or blocks of untested code that are rarely executed pose a lesser threat than complex and frequently executed methods. With limited resources, we would probably want to invest time testing and fixing the second crucial part of source code, rather than the first. Sonar helps in disambiguating such cases.

In this chapter we cover:

- Measuring code coverage
- Code coverage tools
- Code coverage analysis
- Assessing the impact of your tests
- Using the coverage tag cloud component
- jUnit Quickstart
- Reviewing test results in Sonar

Measuring code coverage

Measuring code coverage is essentially the evaluation of how effective our unit or integration tests are and whether they test statements, conditions, and functions for all possible results and arguments. When calculating code coverage, the coverage engine launches test suites with special instrumented code at runtime so as to measure which statements of the code were reached or not.

Some of the basic coverage criteria are as follows:

- **Method coverage**: Call to each method of a class
- **Condition coverage**: Evaluation of Boolean expressions to true or false
- **Decision coverage**: Reach all different branches within a control flow; for example, all cases in a `switch` statement are covered, code tests both `if` and `else` execution paths
- **Statement coverage**: All statements within a method or block were reached by the test suite

Code coverage tools

There are many different code coverage tools specifically for Java, the most popular of them, either free or commercial, being:

- **Cobertura** (free): `http://cobertura.sourceforge.net/`
- **Clover** (Commercial): `http://www.atlassian.com/software/clover/overview`
- **EMMA** (free): `http://emma.sourceforge.net/`
- **JaCoCo** (free): `http://www.eclemma.org/jacoco/`

Sonar uses Cobertura and JaCoCo but there is support for Clover and EMMA via Sonar plugins. The basic lifecycle of a code coverage analysis process consists of the following steps:

- Byte code instrumentation — injects custom code to enable measurements
- Test execution — performs the tests with the injected code
- Analysis report generation — generates a test report in formats such as XML, HTML, PDF
- Sonar data collecting — Sonar collects reporting data

For the needs of the book, we will use the default Cobertura engine.

Performance tests run by the Sonar team on the four tools in 2010 show that Clover is the slower one, consuming twice the time especially when analyzing large projects. Next, we will review all four tools in more detail, and we will also see how we can activate them in Sonar.

 For more information on code coverage tools and their performance, read the excellent article *Pick your code coverage tool in Sonar* by the Sonar team at http://www.sonarsource.org/pick-your-code-coverage-tool-in-sonar-2-2.

Selecting a code coverage tool for Sonar

To review the selected code coverage engine that will process the tests, log in to Sonar as administrator and click on **General Settings** from the left menu to navigate to the Sonar settings screen. From the category column, click on **Code Coverage**. From here, you can view which coverage tool is currently active (default: Cobertura).

To change it, enter the corresponding key value for the desired coverage tool and click on the **Save Code Coverage Settings** button. Notice that EMMA and Clover tools require installing the respective plugins first. You can also override this global setting, by setting a different coverage tool at project level. To do this, navigate to a project's dashboard and click on **Settings** on the left. These configuration settings will override global ones. Then, click on **Code Coverage** and enter the key value that matches the desired code coverage tool to be used for this project.

The four possible key values are as follows:

- `cobertura` — Cobertura (default)
- `clover` — Clover (requires plugin installation first)
- `emma` — EMMA (requires plugin installation first)
- `jacoco` — JaCoCo (it comes preinstalled with Sonar version 2.12+)

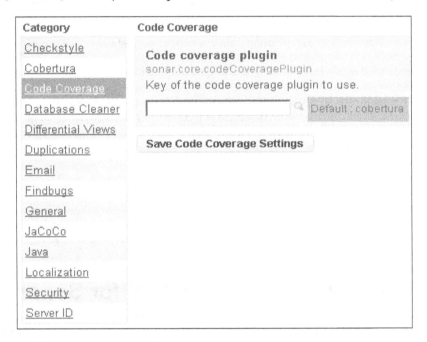

Cobertura

Cobertura is the preselected code coverage tool on a fresh Sonar installation and no additional configuration is necessary, apart from the memory allocation size for the Cobertura processes. The default one at `64m` is enough most of the time, but for large projects with many test suites, it is advisable to increase it to `128m` if applicable.

To change Cobertura memory settings, log in to Sonar as administrator and click on **General Settings** from the menu on the left-hand side. Then, click on the **Cobertura** link to navigate to its configuration screen and enter in the **Maxmem** text field the value 128m. Finally, click on **Save Cobertura Settings** to save.

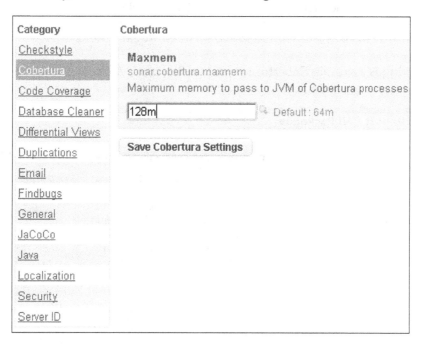

Cobertura is based on the jcoverage tool created by the company jcoverage Ltd and its development has ceased since 2010. Main features of the Cobertura tool are as follows:

- Ant, Maven, and command-line support
- Byte code instrumentation
- Branch coverage
- Report generation in HTML and XML format
- HTML reports support extensive sort functionality per class name/ percentage of lines covered/percentage of branches covered
- Calculate McCabe metric: Cyclomatic code complexity for each class, package, and for the overall product

McCabe metric

The cyclomatic complexity metric was introduced by Thomas McCabe, in an effort to measure complexity of software systems with accuracy. The method calculates complexity about the control flow diagram of the software and directly correlates to it (source: http://en.wikipedia.org/wiki/McCabe_Metric).

The following is a sample Cobertura report (visit http://cobertura.sourceforge.net/sample/ for a live demo):

Coverage Report - All Packages

Package	# Classes	Line Coverage		Branch Coverage		Complexity
All Packages	55	75%	1625/2179	64%	472/738	2.319
net.sourceforge.cobertura.ant	11	52%	170/330	43%	40/94	1.848
net.sourceforge.cobertura.check	3	0%	0/150	0%	0/76	2.429
net.sourceforge.cobertura.coveragedata	13	N/A	N/A	N/A	N/A	2.277
net.sourceforge.cobertura.instrument	10	90%	460/510	75%	123/164	1.854
net.sourceforge.cobertura.merge	1	86%	30/35	88%	14/16	5.5
net.sourceforge.cobertura.reporting	3	87%	116/134	80%	43/54	2.882
net.sourceforge.cobertura.reporting.html	4	91%	475/523	77%	156/202	4.444
net.sourceforge.cobertura.reporting.html.files	1	87%	39/45	62%	5/8	4.5
net.sourceforge.cobertura.reporting.xml	1	100%	155/155	95%	21/22	1.524
net.sourceforge.cobertura.util	9	60%	175/291	69%	70/102	2.892
someotherpackage	1	83%	5/6	N/A	N/A	1.2

JaCoCo

JaCoCo code coverage tool is a subproject of the EclEmma coverage tool for the Eclipse IDE. It is a rather new project and its development is very active. If you develop a project on Eclipse and are interested in code coverage analysis data that is integrated straight into your IDE, visit the EclEmma official website at http://www.eclemma.org.

Since Sonar version 2.12, JaCoCo is preinstalled and you can activate it from the administration settings screen (key value: *jacoco*). Otherwise, the JaCoCo plugin has to be installed first (**Administrator | Update Center | Available Plugins | JaCoCo**). Remember to restart the Sonar server to complete the installation process. In standalone mode, JaCoCo generates a report like the following one (demo report available at `http://www.eclemma.org/jacoco/trunk/coverage/`):

Element	Missed Instructions	Cov.	Missed Branches	Cov.	Missed	Cxty	Missed	Lines
org.jacoco.agent.rt		79%		78%	21	80	41	188
org.jacoco.core		98%		100%	27	696	36	1,648
org.jacoco.ant		93%		90%	13	128	26	387
jacoco-maven-plugin		90%		78%	18	75	12	163
org.jacoco.report		99%		98%	7	446	9	1,164
org.jacoco.agent		85%		75%	3	11	5	33
Total	496 of 14,263	97%	45 of 941	95%	89	1,436	129	3,583

The report includes two more sections displaying coverage data on methods and classes. Each section includes a total coverage percentage, a **Missed** value (for example, how many lines were missed by tests), and complexity for the total complexity of the missed code areas.

Clover Sonar plugin

Clover is a commercial offering by Atlassian (`http://www.atlassian.com/software/clover/overview`) and is available as a Sonar plugin. The main product integrates with Eclipse and IDEA in addition to Ant and Maven plugins. The demo videos at Clover's official page highlight the attention to detail, especially to the user interface. Lots of information are organized within intuitive screens. If you want to see it in action, you can download a free 30-day trial version and see for yourself.

If you have purchased a Clover license key and want to use it in Sonar, you will have to install the Sonar Clover plugin from the Update Center. Once the installation process is complete, restart the server and go to **Configuration | General Settings | Clover**. Fill in the **License** text field with your license key and click on **Save Clover Settings**. Next, click on the **Code Coverage** link, fill in the **Key** text field with the value clover, and click **Save Code Coverage Settings**.

Clover

License
sonar.clover.license.secured
You can obtain a free 30 day evaluation license or purchase a commercial license at http://my.atlassian.com.

Clover version
sonar.clover.version
Override the Clover version to use. Default value is read from pom, else 3.0.5

Report path
sonar.clover.reportPath
Absolute or relative path to XML report file.

Save Clover Settings

Emma Sonar plugin

Emma is a free code coverage tool and came to life back in 2005. Development has now ceased with a final release in June 2005. To use Emma in Sonar, go to **General Settings** from **Administration** and set the **Code Coverage** property value to emma.

A brief overview of Emma features:

- Byte code instrumentation, both offline and at runtime
- Coverage at line, block, method, and class level
- Coverage stats from method to package level
- Report generation in HTML and XML format
- Works in any Java 2 JVM (1.2+)

The following screen is a sample Emma coverage report for the Apache Velocity version 1.4 project:

name	class, %		method, %		block, %		line, %	
EMMA Coverage Report (generated Tue May 18 22:20:04 CDT 2004)								
[all classes]								
OVERALL COVERAGE SUMMARY								
name	class, %		method, %		block, %		line, %	
all classes	98%	(118/120)	66%	(318/483)	81%	(15517/19107)	77%	(2651.4/3430)
OVERALL STATS SUMMARY								

```
OVERALL STATS SUMMARY

total packages:          1
total executable files:  31
total classes:           120
total methods:           483
total executable lines:  3430
```

COVERAGE BREAKDOWN BY PACKAGE

name	class, %		method, %		block, %		line, %	
default package	98%	(118/120)	66%	(318/483)	81%	(15517/19107)	77%	(2651.4/343

[all classes]

EMMA 2.0.4015 (stable) (C) Vladimir Roubtsov

The report consolidates coverage percentage data into four different sections for each level respectively — class, method, block, and line. For more sample reports, visit Emma's official site at http://emma.sourceforge.net/samples.html.

Code coverage analysis

To better understand how Sonar works and to be in a position to better evaluate code coverage results, it is necessary to take a closer look at how code coverage tools analyze tests and calculate total coverage. The result of the coverage analysis process, although expressed as a single percentage number in Sonar, is based on many different coverage metrics.

Next, we will examine four fundamental coverage metrics used by all code coverage tools supported by Sonar:

- Statement coverage
- Branch coverage (also known as **decision coverage**)
- Condition coverage
- Path coverage

Statement coverage

Statement coverage is the most basic metric of the analysis process. It is the building block element for the rest of the metrics. The metric reports whether a statement was encountered during test execution. Usually, statements and lines coincide, thus the metric is also known as **line coverage**. Once a line of code is encountered, it is considered as covered. This has the side effect of not taking into account the possibility of different execution paths for control flow statements such as the `if else` blocks.

For example, consider the following block of code:

```
if (condition) {
  ...
  ...  // 99 statements in total
  ...
} else {
  ... // one single statement
}
```

If during unit testing, `condition` always evaluates to `true` then the statement coverage metric will report 99 percent coverage, missing the single statement inside the `else` block. This 99 percent is misleading though as the `else` execution path is left out from unit tests completely.

Branch/decision coverage

Branch or decision coverage expands on statement coverage by reporting whether `Boolean` expressions were tested sufficiently — evaluated to `true` or `false` — so as to enable all possible execution paths in control structures.

For example, branch coverage reports a 100 percent result when a unit test's condition evaluates to `true` in one case and `false` in another.

```
if (condition) {
  . . .
} else {
  . . .
}
```

Condition coverage

Condition coverage reports on the `true` or `false` outcome of an expression. To report 100 percent, all the operands of the expression must be tested for all possible values. The only disadvantage of this metric is that it does not guarantee that all edges of the program will be visited. For example, an expression evaluates always to `true` or `false` regardless of the operand values. Combining condition coverage with decision coverage resolves this issue.

Path coverage

Path coverage is the most thorough metric because it tests whether all possible combinations of control flow were visited during unit testing from the entry point of a method to the exit.

For example, in the following block of code, path coverage will report four different unique execution paths:

```
if (conditionA) {
    ...

    if (conditionB){
        ...
    } else {
        ...
    }

} else {
    ...
}
```

Adding another `if else` block would raise the total paths exponentially to a total of 8.

Assessing the impact of your tests

After a Sonar analysis, the first place to review testing coverage is within the project dashboard. A dedicated widget reports total coverage in percentage form, breaking down to line and branch coverage as shown in the following screenshot:

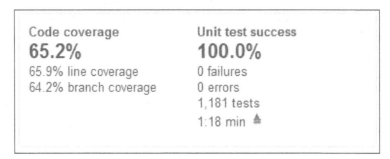

Click on any metric from the left widget section to drill down to package level. Packages are listed along with the coverage metric as a percentage and clicking on them lists their respective classes and coverage value on the right side of the panel.

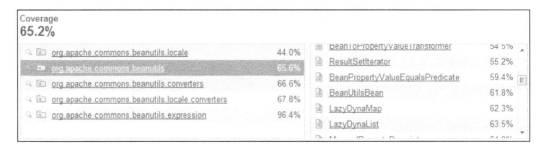

Click on a class to open the Sonar source viewer with focus on the coverage tab. You can view a summary of the following metrics at the top of the tab for the corresponding class. Below the metrics, you can select from the menu on the right which parts of the source are displayed, for example, the lines or branches to cover.

- Line coverage – in percentage
- Branch coverage – in percentage
- Uncovered lines – absolute values
- Uncovered branches – absolute values

Statements reached by a unit test are covered and highlighted with a green number. The number for single statements is one. For control flow statements, it is higher depending on the number of the conditions. For a single Boolean expression, there are two conditions to cover, `true` and `false`, and the number has a maximum value of two, meaning that there are two paths that must be covered by unit tests..

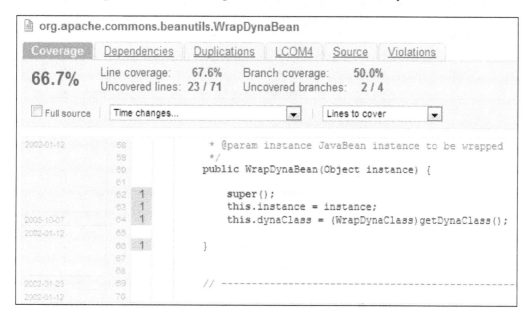

Uncovered lines

Uncovered statements are highlighted in red. In the following screen, we see that both `if else` blocks and inner statements are untested. Because neither clause is ever visited, the number in red is two, which means that the block was not tested at all.

Uncovered branches

In cases where branches were covered partially and not tested for all possible outcomes, Sonar highlights them with a yellow number, denoting the number of the conditions that were covered. For example, an expression with two Boolean conditions allows four possible combinations. A yellow number 3 means that one combination was never tested. The green number on the left simply means that the line was reached.

```
1117            * @return The cost of transforming an object
1118            */
1119           private static float getObjectTransformationCost(Class srcClass, Class destClass) {
1120               float cost = 0.0f;
1121    1   3/4       while (srcClass != null && !destClass.equals(srcClass)) {
1122                      if (destClass.isPrimitive()) {
1123                          Class destClassWrapperClazz = getPrimitiveWrapper(destClass);
1124    1   2/4           if (destClassWrapperClazz != null && destClassWrapperClazz.equals(srcClass)) {
1125                              cost += 0.25f;
1126                              break;
1127                          }
1128                      }
1129    1   3/4           if (destClass.isInterface() && isAssignmentCompatible(destClass,srcClass)) {
1130                          // slight penalty for interface match.
1131                          // we still want an exact match to override an interface match, but
1132                          // an interface match should override anything where we have to get a
1133                          // superclass.
```

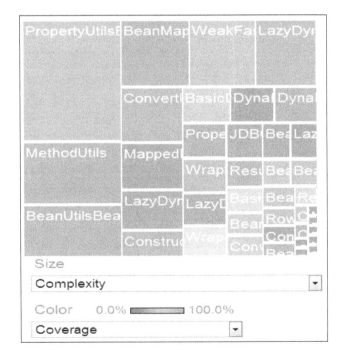

Using the coverage tag cloud component

The coverage cloud component provides information in a quick and efficient way. Java classes are represented as tags a in tag cloud, while tag colors and font sizes correspond to different metrics depending on the selected mode: **Quick wins** or **Top risk**.

To view the coverage cloud, visit the dashboard of a project, click on the link **Clouds** from the menu on the left, and set the **Color** property to **Coverage**. The following screenshot shows the coverage cloud for the Apache Commons library. Mouse over a class to get metric values or click on its tag to open it in the Sonar source viewer.

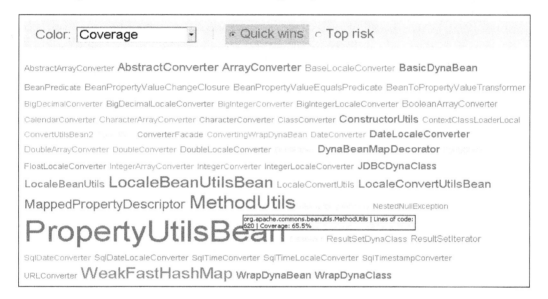

Quick wins mode

In Quick wins mode, the coverage cloud represents:

- Font size: Total lines of code
- Color: Code coverage ranging from red (0 percent) to blue (100 percent)

Top risk mode

In Top risk mode, the coverage cloud represents:

- Font size: Average complexity/method (absolute value)
- Color: Code coverage ranging from red (0 percent) to blue (100 percent)

Where to start testing

The coverage cloud proves to be a great tool when it comes to deciding what tests to write next, since the visual representation allows quick comparisons at a glance. Writing tests with no real value to the software product, only to technically increase coverage, is not uncommon. It is essential that unit tests are written from a production perspective in an effort to simulate real-case scenarios and method calls.

The Top risk approach

Switching to Top risk mode, we are presented with a cloud that is substantially different from the Quick wins one. It is recommended to use this view, as it takes into account the complexity of each class irrespective of the line count. It is more important to provide tests for complex methods that control and dictate the program flow, and take care of standalone statements later.

The following screen is the same as the previous one, the only difference being that it is switched to Top risk mode. Obviously, the clouds are quite different. After examining the second one, a quick assessment would be that converters lack coverage in general and should be tested extensively since they are fairly complex classes.

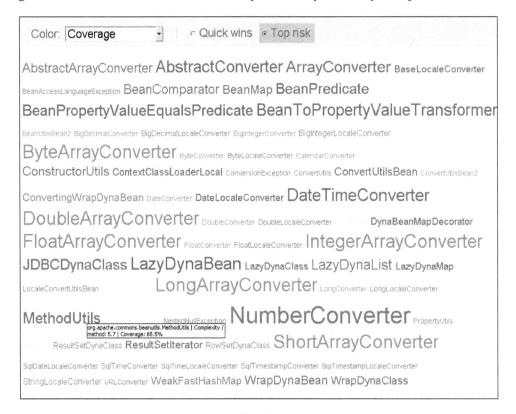

jUnit Quickstart

jUnit is a framework for writing and running test cases—`http://junit.org/`.
A test is a Java class containing jUnit annotations to set up the test and identify test methods. Basically, you annotate test methods with the `@Test` annotation and verify results using assertion. When you want to check a value dependent on the nature of the check and the type of the value, you call the appropriate assertion.

For example, if you want to check that the value of a Boolean variable is `true`, you would write: `assertTrue(var)`. There are many different assertions located in package import `org.junit.Assert.*`. Notice that you have to import this package statically to each test class. Methods containing test code are annotated with `@org.junit.Test`. For example:

```
@Test
public void testFoo(){
  ..
}
```

To start writing your own tests, download `junit-4.xx.jar` from `https://github.com/KentBeck/junit/downloads` and add it to the class path.

Writing a simple unit test

Next, we will go through a basic test example and use the most important jUnit annotations such as:

* `@Before`

* `@After`

* `@Test`

* `@Test(expected = parameter)`

Consider the following simple `Calculator.java` class:

```
/*
 * Calculator.java
 */

public class Calculator {

    /**
     * Converts passed arguments to integers
     * and performs addition.
     * @param stra first argument
     * @param strb second argument
     * @return addition result of arguments
     * @throws NumberFormatException
```

```
    */
    public int addition(final String stra,
            final String strb)
        throws NumberFormatException{
        final int a = Integer.valueOf(stra);
        final int b = Integer.valueOf(strb);
        return a + b;
    }
}
```

And its corresponding annotated `CalculatorTest.java` test case:

```java
import org.junit.After;
import org.junit.Before;
import org.junit.Test;

import junit.framework.TestCase;

/* CalculatorTest.java
 */
public class CalculatorTest extends TestCase {

    private Calculator calculator;

    public CalculatorTest(String name) {
        super(name);
    }

    @Before
    public void setUp()  {
        calculator = new Calculator();
    }

    @After
    public void tearDown()  {
        calculator = null;
    }

    @Test
    public void testAddition(){
        String stra = "2";
        String strb = "3";
        int expected = 5;
        int actual = calculator.addition(stra, strb);
        assertEquals(expected, actual);
    }

    @Test(expected = NumberFormatException.class)
    public void testAdditionEx(){
        String stra = "str";
        String strb = "3";
        calculator.addition(stra, strb);
    }

}
```

The `CalculatorTest` class declares a `Calculator` field and two methods, which test the `addition` method. Before we start executing test methods, we have to initialize the calculator inside the `setUp` method. The `setUp` method annotated with `@Before` will be conveniently invoked before any actual testing takes place. Similarly, the `@After` annotation causes the `tearDown` method to be invoked after the testing is complete and is responsible for cleaning up resources.

The next two methods `testAddition` and `testAdditionEx` are annotated with `@Test` and this is where the testing code resides. The `Calculator` field has already been initialized, and therefore we can use it now for testing purposes.

The first method simply tests the result of *2 + 3* and performs `assertEquals` to check whether the return value is *5*. However, at runtime, there is the potential of passing invalid `String` arguments, for example not numbers, causing `NumberFormatException` to be thrown. To cover this possibility for testing purposes, we can pass invalid arguments and verify that a `NumberFormatException` exception is thrown by the program. We can achieve this by defining the expected parameter of the `@Test` annotation equal to `NumberFormatException.class` and write code that intentionally throws this exception. This is a common practice to test exception handling and verify correct program behavior.

Reviewing test results in Sonar

When unit tests fail and success rate falls below 100 percent, the code coverage widget highlights the percentage value to notify us that something did not test as expected. Below the percentile value, you can view the number of total test failures. A failure means that a method inside a test annotated with `@Test` did not pass the assertion check. Click on the percentage value or the **failures** number to get an overview of the affected classes. From there you can drill down from package level to class level and pinpoint the failing test. The numbers next to packages, classes, or methods are the total number of failures at the respective level.

Code coverage
34.4%
36.3% line coverage
29.1% branch coverage

Unit test success
98.2%
1 failures
0 errors
57 tests
1:13 min

When you click on test class, the Sonar source viewer opens below the drill down panel with focus on the **Tests** tab. The header of the tab includes the following information from left to right:

- Test success rate as percentile value
- Total number of tests executed
- Total number of failures
- Total test duration in seconds

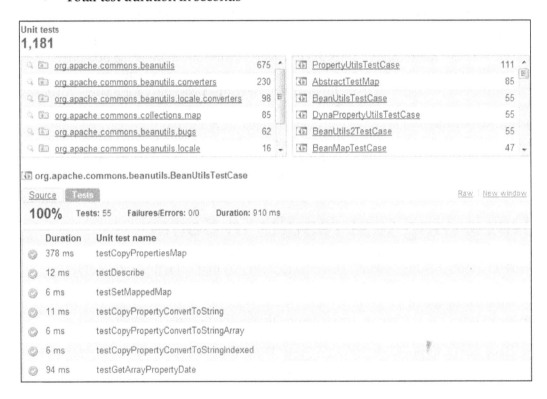

In this example, the test method `testSSlHtmlConnection()` has failed and therefore it is specifically highlighted, as shown in the following screenshot:

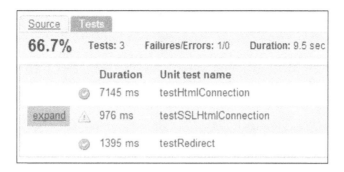

Whenever a test fails due to assertion failure, jUnit logs a message with the expected and actual values in order to assist the developer understand what went wrong. Click on the **expand** link to review the assertion message. For `assertEquals()`, the output would be similar to the following code:

```
expected:<1> but was:<0>
junit.framework.AssertionFailedError: expected:<1> but was:<0>
at junit.framework.Assert.fail(Assert.java:47)
at junit.framework.Assert.failNotEquals(Assert.java:277)
at junit.framework.Assert.assertEquals(Assert.java:64)
at junit.framework.Assert.assertEquals(Assert.java:195)
at junit.framework.Assert.assertEquals(Assert.java:201)
at org.apache.ahc.MonitoringTest.testSSLHtmlConnection(MonitoringTest.
java:70)
```

Summary

In this chapter, we discussed what code coverage is and reviewed the tools that Sonar uses to perform such an analysis. After a more detailed look at specific coverage metrics such as decision, condition, and path coverage, we examined the Sonar interface and how it helps us identify complex classes lacking tests. Finally, we covered basic concepts of the jUnit testing library as a first step towards unit test writing.

In the next chapter, we will review the process of creating an integrated development environment complete with a source code repository, a build server, and Sonar according to the continuous inspection paradigm.

11
Integrating Sonar

In this chapter, we will discuss continuous integration and inspection processes and set up a continuous integration environment to enable these practices. We will install **Software Configuration Management (SCM)**, and learn how to import and manage the source code hosted in it. Then, we will install the Jenkins Continuous Integration server (Jenkins CI) and connect a project in the repository to the build server to automate the build process. Finally, we will install the Jenkins Sonar plugin and configure a build job in Jenkins so as to automatically execute a Sonar analysis after each build.

In this chapter, we cover:

- The Continuous Inspection paradigm
- Installing Subversion
- Setting up a Subversion server
- Installing Jenkins CI Server
- Configuring Jenkins
- Creating a build job
- Installing the Sonar plugin
- Building and monitoring your project

The Continuous Inspection paradigm

Continuous integration is a software development practice where team developers integrate their code frequently. Each time a change is committed to the source code a new build is provided, usually through an automated process. The project grows incrementally, a stable build is always available for every iteration, and build errors can be identified by team members quickly.

Foundation. A central Subversion server manages different versions of files/projects,
while developers connect to the server via command line or GUI tools to commit
their changes to the code. For more information on Subversion, visit the project's
home page at http://subversion.apache.org/.

For the needs of the book, we will only use basic commands to import a project into
Subversion and commit changes to files. To learn more about Subversion, download
the free book *Version Control with Subversion* from http://svnbook.red-bean.com/
or visit Apache's Subversion documentation page at http://subversion.apache.
org/docs/.

Next, we will install the Subversion server and its client on Linux and Windows.

Ubuntu/Debian Subversion installation

Ubuntu and Debian distributions maintain Subversion projects and are available within the Synaptic Package Manager tool. To install both the Subversion server and client, open a terminal and enter the following commands:

```
$ sudo apt-get install subversion
$ sudo apt-get install libapache2-svn
```

For more information on Debian Subversion packages visit
http://packages.debian.org/search?keywords=subversion&exact=1.

Ubuntu Subversion package information can be found at
http://packages.ubuntu.com/search?keywords=subversion&exact=1.

Red Hat Subversion installation

For Red Hat Linux, you can choose between three different releases, namely Redhat standard Subversion package, WANdisco, or SummerSoft. WANdisco provides one release to cover all Red Hat versions and requires registration, while SummerSoft hosts multiple rpm packages and does not require registration.

To install Redhat's standard Subversion package, open the terminal and enter the following command as root:

```
# yum install mod_dav_svn subversion
```

If you don't have Apache installed already, this command also installs it.

To install the SummerSoft release, visit http://the.earth.li/pub/subversion/ summersoft.fay.ar.us/pub/subversion/latest/, select the directory with the highest version number, and download and install the rpm package for your Red Hat distribution.

To install WANdisco's release go to http://www.wandisco.com/subversion/ download#redhat and click on the **Download Subversion Installer** link. Complete the registration form and download the installer. Then, open a terminal and enter the following commands as root:

```
# chmod +x svninstall_rhel5_wandisco.sh
# ./svninstall_rhel5_wandisco.sh
```

If you wish to update your installation, you can at any time use the yum update command:

```
# yum upgrade
```

Installing Subversion on other Linux distributions

If you wish to install Subversion on a Linux distribution not covered here, visit Apache's official page for a comprehensive list and installation instructions on all supported Subversion binary packages at `http://subversion.apache.org/packages.html`.

Windows Subversion installation

For Windows we will install *CollabNet's Subversion Edge 2.3.0.*

Visit `http://www.open.collab.net/downloads/subversion/`, and scroll down to find the *CollabNet Subversion Edge 2.3.0* sections for Windows 32-bit or 64-bit.

Click on the **Download** button to register for a CollabNet account and when the download is complete, run the installer. After the installation process has finished, you will have a new Subversion service running, ready to host repositories.

More Windows Subversion installation binaries are available at `http://subversion.apache.org/packages.html#windows`.

Setting up a Subversion server

Next, we will create a repository for our projects, configure a user named `svnpackt` to have access to the repository, and import a dummy Maven project named `packt-app` into the repository. The process is the same for Linux and Windows.

Creating a Subversion repository

A Subversion repository is simply a directory in the filesystem containing repository configuration files and our project's files. To create a repository, open a terminal and enter the following command:

```
$ svnadmin create $PATH_REPO
```

Replace `$PATH_REPO` with a directory, for example, `/home/dev/repo`.

To verify the creation of the repository, navigate to $PATH_REPO. The following directories should have been created:

- `conf`: Subversion configuration files
- `db`: Project data files and revisions
- `hooks`: Templates for useful automation commands
- `locks`: Logs of locked files, checked out and modified by developers
- `format` (file): Contains information about the repository's layout
- README.txt (file): Getting started configuration information

Subversion security and authorization

Subversion supports different authorization schemes, with the simplest one being password-file-based authentication. User names and passwords are stored in a `passwd` file stored inside the repository's `conf` directory. Navigate to the `$PATH_REPO/conf` directory, open the `svnserve.conf` file, and uncomment the line `password-db = passwd`:

```
### If SASL is enabled (see below), this file will NOT be used.
### Uncomment the line below to use the default password file.
password-db = passwd
```

To create the user `svnpackt` with password `svnpackt`, open the `passwd` file inside the `$PATH_REPO/conf` directory and add the line `svnpackt = svnpackt`:

```
[users]
# harry = harryssecret
# sally = sallyssecret
svnpackt = svnpackt
```

Importing a project into Subversion

To create a simple Maven project, open the terminal and enter the following command:

```
mvn archetype:generate \
  -DarchetypeGroupId=org.apache.maven.archetypes \
  -DgroupId=com.packt.app \
  -DartifactId=packt-app
```

Notice that the previous command is a single line broken down with backslashes only for formatting purposes. You should enter it as one line, omitting the backslashes.

Maven will start downloading the necessary archetype definition files, and eventually you will be prompted to choose the version of the quickstart Maven archetype to use:

```
1: 1.0-alpha-1
2: 1.0-alpha-2
3: 1.0-alpha-3
4: 1.0-alpha-4
5: 1.0
6: 1.1

Choose a number: 6: 6
```

Enter 6 and press *Enter* to continue.

```
[INFO] Using property: groupId = com.packt.app
[INFO] Using property: artifactId = packt-app
Define value for property 'version':  1.0-SNAPSHOT: : 1.0
```

When prompted for version, type 1.0 and then hit *Enter*.

```
Confirm properties configuration:
groupId: com.packt.app
artifactId: packt-app
version: 1.0
package: com.packt.app
Y: : Y
```

Finally, press *Y* to complete the process. Maven has created the `packt-app` project directory along with all necessary directories. The project contains one `main` class, in package `com.packt.app`:

```java
package com.packt.app;

/**
 * Hello world!
 *
 */
public class App
{
    public static void main( String[] args )
    {
        System.out.println( "Hello World!" );
    }
}
```

Before we import the project into Subversion, we must create a `packt-app` directory within the repository. To do this, enter the following commands—the first one is to start the Subversion server in case it is not running. When prompted for password, enter `svnpackt`. Remember to replace the `$PATH_REPO` variable with the real location of the repository in your system.

```
$ svnserve -d
$ svn mkdir svn://localhost/$PATH_REPO/packt-app --username svnpackt

..

Store password unencrypted (yes/no)? yes
Committed revision 1.
```

Next, open a terminal and change directory (`cd`) to one level up from where the `packt-app` directory was created earlier by Maven. You should be able to list the directory by typing `ls` in Linux or `dir` in Windows.

Then, enter the following command to import the project into Subversion:

```
$ svn import packt-app svn://localhost/$PATH_REPO/packt-app --username
svnpackt
Adding              packt-app/src
Adding              packt-app/src/test
Adding              packt-app/src/test/java
Adding              packt-app/src/test/java/com
Adding              packt-app/src/test/java/com/packt

...

Adding              packt-app/src/main/java/com/packt/app/App.java
Adding              packt-app/pom.xml
Committed revision 2.
```

Now that the `packt-app` project is stored into the Subversion repository, we can delete the local copy and check it out again directly from the server. Open the terminal, change directory (`cd`) to where you want to check out the project, and enter the following command:

```
$ svn co svn://localhost/$PATH_REPO/packt-app
A    packt-app/src
A    packt-app/src/test
A    packt-app/src/test/java
A    packt-app/src/test/java/com
A    packt-app/src/test/java/com/packt
```

```
A     packt-app/src/test/java/com/packt/app
A     packt-app/src/test/java/com/packt/app/AppTest.java
A     packt-app/src/main
A     packt-app/src/main/java
A     packt-app/src/main/java/com
A     packt-app/src/main/java/com/packt
A     packt-app/src/main/java/com/packt/app
A     packt-app/src/main/java/com/packt/app/App.java
A     packt-app/pom.xml
Checked out revision 2.
```

Whenever you want to commit changes or execute Subversion commands regarding the project, open a terminal within the project's directory and enter them from there. For example, invoking `svn` with the `info` parameter inside the `packt-app` directory lists the following information:

```
$ svn info
    Path: .
    URL: svn://localhost/$PATH_REPO/packt-app
    Repository Root: svn://$PATH_REPO
    Repository UUID: 376b09b6-4792-4d11-81d4-d4c6ca5824dc
    Revision: 2
    Node Kind: directory
    Schedule: normal
    Last Changed Author: svnpackt
    Last Changed Rev: 2
```

Installing the Jenkins CI server

The Jenkins Continuous Integration server, formerly known as Hudson before the renaming of the project took place, has been created by Kohsuke Kawaguchi. The official site of the project is available at `http://jenkins-ci.org/`. At the end of the installation process, you will have a running Jenkins server at `http://localhost:8080/`.

Here is how the welcome page looks:

Ubuntu/Debian Jenkins installation

Enter the following command to add the necessary key for the Jenkins Debian package repository:

```
$ wget -q -O - http://pkg.jenkins-ci.org/debian/jenkins-ci.org.key | sudo
apt-key add -
```

To add the repository, add the following APT line entry in your /etc/apt/ sources.list:

```
deb http://pkg.jenkins-ci.org/debian binary/
```

Alternatively, you can run the Synaptic Package Manager tool and select **Repositories** from the **Settings** menu. Select the **Third-Party Software** tab and click on the **Add** button to enter the repository's APT line. Click on **Add Source** and **Close** to close the **Repositories** pop-up:

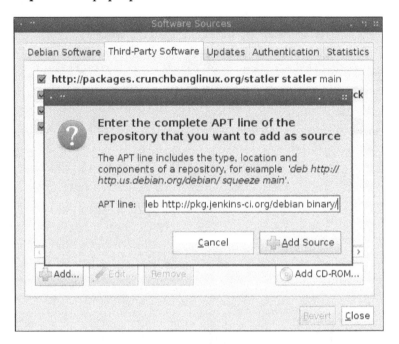

Finally, open a terminal and enter the following commands to perform the installation:

```
$ sudo apt-get update
$ sudo apt-get install jenkins
```

When the installation process completes, navigate to `http://localhost:8080/` to verify that Jenkins is up and running.

As for the Jenkins service, it is good to know that:

- Jenkins will be launched as a daemon up on start. See `/etc/init.d/jenkins` for more details.
- The Jenkins user is created to run this service.
- Log files will be placed in `/var/log/jenkins/jenkins.log`. Check this file if you are troubleshooting Jenkins.

For more information, visit Jenkins's Ubuntu installation wiki at `https://wiki.jenkins-ci.org/display/JENKINS/Installing+Jenkins+on+Ubuntu`.

Redhat/Fedora/CentOS Jenkins installation

To use the Jenkins `rpm` repository, open a terminal and enter the following commands:

```
sudo wget -O /etc/yum.repos.d/jenkins.repo http://pkg.jenkins-ci.org/
redhat/jenkins.repo
sudo rpm --import http://pkg.jenkins-ci.org/redhat/jenkins-ci.org.key
```

Then, the Jenkins package can be installed with:

```
$ yum install jenkins
```

When the installation process completes, navigate to `http://localhost:8080/` to verify that Jenkins is up and running.

To start, stop, or restart the service use:

```
$ sudo service jenkins start/stop/restart
```

The Jenkins service runs as follows:

- Jenkins will be launched as a daemon up on start. See `/etc/init.d/jenkins` for more details.
- The Jenkins user is created to run this service.
- Log files will be placed in `/var/log/jenkins/jenkins.log`. Check this file if you are troubleshooting Jenkins.

For more information, visit Jenkins's RedHat installation wiki at `https://wiki.jenkins-ci.org/display/JENKINS/Installing+Jenkins+on+Red Hat+distributions`.

Windows Jenkins installation

Download and run the Jenkins installer from `http://mirrors.jenkins-ci.org/windows/latest` to install Jenkins as a Windows service configured to start automatically upon boot. To start/stop it manually, use the service manager from the control panel, or the `sc` command-line tool.

When the installation process completes, navigate to `http://localhost:8080/` to verify that Jenkins is up and running.

Configuring Jenkins

Ensure that the Jenkins service is running and go to `http://localhost:8080/`.
From there, click on the **Manage Jenkins** link on the left menu to view the list of
links leading to different configuration pages. Click on the top one, **Configure
System**, to navigate to the configuration dashboard. This dashboard features
many different sections which we will configure one by one.

JDK configuration

Click on the **Add JDK** button to expand this section. If your installed JDK has not
been auto-detected by Jenkins, you have to enter it manually in the **Name** field.
Unless, of course, you want Jenkins to install JDK automatically for you, in which
case you check the **Install automatically** checkbox.

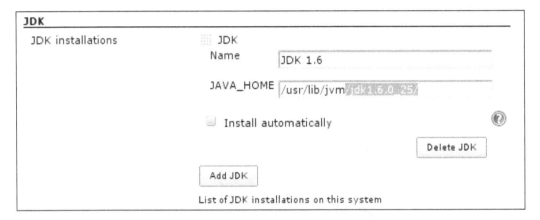

Maven configuration

Click on the **Add Maven** button and fill in the **Name** and **MAVEN_HOME** fields to match your own Maven installation. Jenkins will use this Maven installation to execute builds. Alternatively, you can check the **Install automatically** checkbox and have Jenkins install it automatically from Apache.

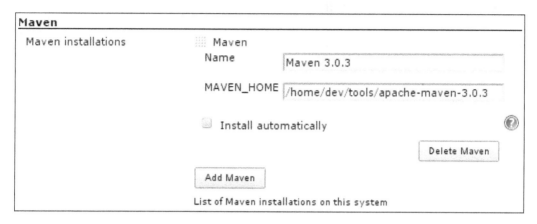

Repository configuration

Next, configure the Subversion section as shown in the following screen:

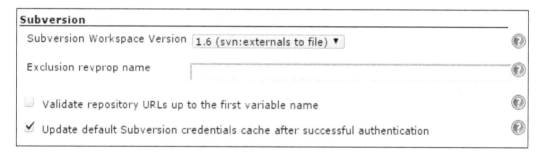

E-mail server configuration

Jenkins supports user notification on various build events such as *build failed* or *build restored*. To enable the notification support, you have to configure the SMTP server and SMPT authentication if applicable—check your e-mail server settings before making changes to this section. The **Sender E-mail Address** field value will be the address Jenkins will use to e-mail users.

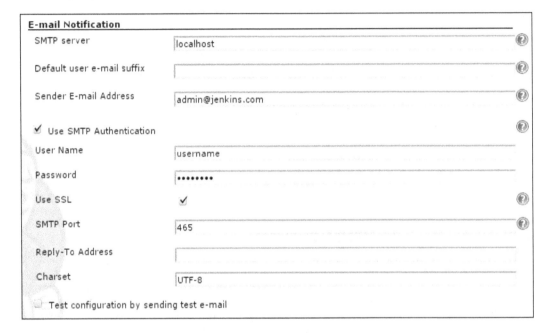

Securing Jenkins

By default, Jenkins is open for use and configuration by anyone, requiring no authentication. Scroll up to the top and check the **Enable Security** checkbox to expand the security configuration section.

From **Security Realm**, select **Jenkins's own user database** and if you wish, check the **Allow users to sign up** checkbox.

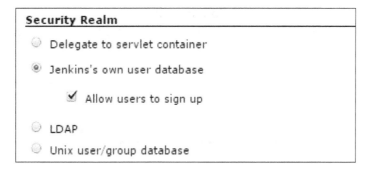

Click on the **Matrix-based security** radio button, type packt in the **User/group to add** input field, and click on the **Add** button. On the new row, check all the privileges to make sure that this user has rights to everything.

Finally, click on the **Save** button to preserve configuration changes and click again on the top-left Jenkins logo to return home. Now, you will be prompted to log in. Do not log in, click on the **Create Account** link instead, and fill in the form with your account details entering packt as the username. Afterwards, you will be able to log in with your packt account normally.

Creating a build job

Next, we will create a new build job for the packt-app Maven project. Log in to Jenkins and click on the **New Job** link from the left. Enter a job name and select the **maven2/3** radio button. Then, click on **OK** to proceed to the job's configuration screen.

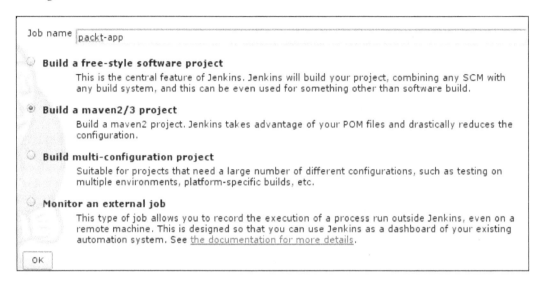

Click on the **Subversion** radio button and enter the **Repository URL** of the packt project. Remember to replace the $PATH_REPO environment variable with the repository directory as it is configured in your own system. Leave the rest of the fields to their default values.

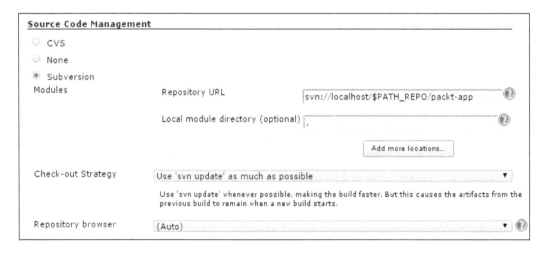

Configure the **Build Triggers** section as shown in the following screenshot:

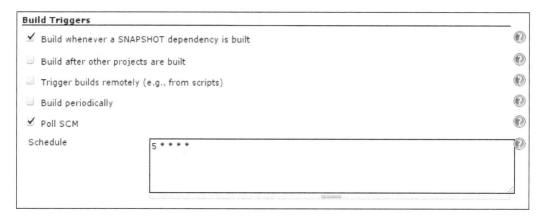

The **Poll SCM** value 5 * * * * is a cron expression and means that Jenkins will poll the Subversion server every five minutes and if any changes are detected, it will update the source code to pull the changes and automatically execute the packt-app build job. Click on the question mark beside the **Poll SCM** field for more configuration options.

Cron expression and scheduling

Cron is a time-based job scheduler in Unix operating systems that allows you to schedule jobs using expressions. A cron expression is a string of five fields with each field representing a different unit of time as follows:

- **Minutes**: 0-59
- **Hours**: 0-23
- **Day of month**: 0-23, use ? if not applicable
- **Month**: 1-12
- **Day of week**: 0-6 or SUN-SAT (by name)

Take a look at the following examples:

- 0 5 ? * MON (every Monday at 05:00 AM)
- 30 18 * * ? (every day at 06:00 PM)

Finally, click on the **Save** button and navigate back to the Jenkins home page by clicking on the top-left logo. Your new job now appears in the job list at the center of the page. You can click on the rightmost play button to start the job, or click on the job's name—for example, **packt-app**—to go to the dashboard. To reconfigure the job, click on **Configure** from the menu on the left. To browse build artifacts, click on **Workspace**.

Installing the Sonar plugin

Before we test our new job, let's install the Sonar plugin. The Sonar plugin enables Jenkins to initiate a Sonar analysis after each build. From the Jenkins home page `http://localhost:8080/`, click on the **Manage Jenkins** link, and **Manage Plugins** from the next screen. Click on the **Available** tab and search (*Ctrl + F*) for Sonar to find and select the Sonar plugin. Then, click on the **Install without restart** button to start the installation process.

While Jenkins is downloading and installing the plugin, make sure to check the **Restart Jenkins** option as shown in the following screenshot. This will ensure that Jenkins restarts immediately once the installation is complete.

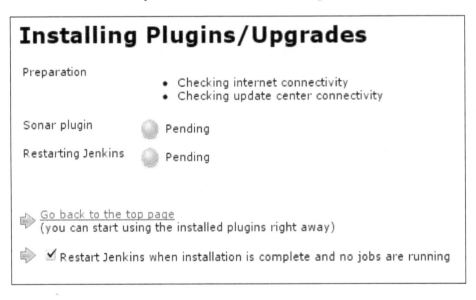

With the Sonar plugin installed, go to **Manage Jenkins | Configure System** and scroll down to the Sonar section. Provide a name for the Sonar server and click on **Save**. If the Sonar server is installed at a URL other than the default one (`http://localhost:9000/`), click on the **Advanced...** button and enter your Sonar server's URL in the Server URL input field.

Sonar

Sonar installations	Name	SonarServer
	Disable	☐
		Check to quickly disable Sonar on all jobs.

Add Sonar

List of Sonar installations

Next, we will enable the Sonar analysis as a post-build action for our `packt-app` job. Go back to the Jenkins home page and from the job list, select the **packt-app** job by clicking on its name. Click on **Configure** from the left menu and scroll down to the bottom of the page. Check the **Sonar** checkbox from the **Post-build Actions** section to enable Sonar analysis. Hover over the question mark icons for information on the rest of the options — archive the build artifact, build other dependent projects, install the artifact to a Maven artifact repository, and so on. Additionally, you can enable **E-mail Notification** and provide a list of user's e-mails to notify whenever a build event is triggered by this build job.

Finally, click on **Save** to preserve your changes and return to the job's dashboard.

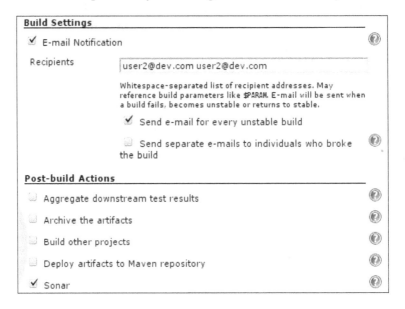

Building and monitoring your project

To test our new job, go to the Jenkins homepage at `http://localhost:8080/` and click on the play button, as shown in the following screenshot, to execute the building process. The **Build Executor Status** panel on the left of the page displays the progress of the build. You can click on the build number and then on the **Console Output** link on the left to inspect the build log as it runs. Notice that after the build completes, a Sonar analysis is triggered and executed.

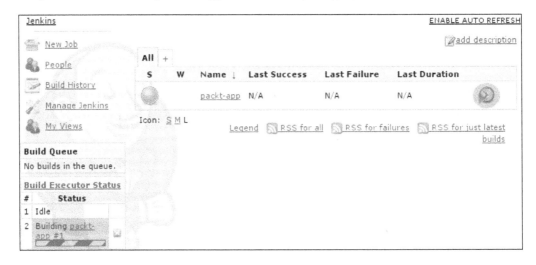

Once the build has finished successfully, the status of the job turns blue. Click on the project's name to navigate to the details page.

From here, you can access all past build data, download build artifacts, and review test results. Click on the **Workspace** link to download artifacts and review the build logs.

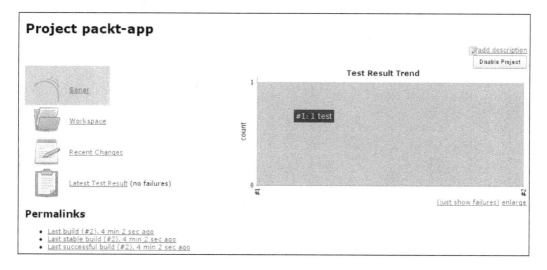

Click the **Sonar** link to go straight to the project's Sonar dashboard:

Summary

In this chapter, we went through the process of setting up and configuring an integrated build and quality analysis environment. We installed Subversion, Jenkins Continuous Integration server, and the necessary Sonar plugin.

We configured Jenkins to poll the source code repository and execute a build process and Sonar analysis whenever changes are detected. From now on, every time a developer commits a change to the repository, a new build and Sonar analysis will be available.

Sonar Metrics Index

This appendix lists all Sonar metrics in separate categories along with a brief description for each metric and information on where to locate it within the Sonar user interface.

Sonar metrics

Sonar metrics are categorized into the following categories:

- Complexity
- Design and Architecture
- Documentation
- Duplication
- General
- Unit Tests
- Rules Compliance and Violations
- Project Size
- Management

Complexity metrics

Complexity metrics are available in the Complexity and Quality Index widgets in the dashboard. The Quality Index widget is available as a plugin.

Metric name	Definition	Sonar component
Complexity	The total Cyclomatic Complexity number was introduced by McCabe. For each of the following java statements the number increments by one: `if, for, while, case, catch, throw, return, &&, ||,` and `?`.	This is available via the **Complexity widget**. Navigate to **Dashboard** | **Complexity Widget** | **Total**.
Complexity / class	Average Cyclomatic Complexity per class.	This is available via the **Complexity widget**. Navigate to **Dashboard** | **Complexity widget** | **Per Class metric**.
Complexity / file	Average Cyclomatic Complexity per file.	This is available via the **Complexity widget**. Navigate to **Dashboard** | **Complexity widget** | **Per File metric**.
Complexity / method	Average Cyclomatic Complexity per method.	This is available via the **Complexity** widget. Navigate to **Dashboard** | **Complexity widget** | **Per Method metric**.
Complexity Factor	Density of complexity in methods in percentage.	This is available via the **Quality Index** widget. Navigate to **Dashboard** | **Quality Index** widget | **Complexity factor percentage**.
Complexity Factor Methods	Methods with high complexity density.	These are available via the **Quality Index** widget. Navigate to **Dashboard** | **Quality Index** widget | **Complexity Factor Methods total**.
QI Complexity	Complexity rating in respect to total LOC.	This is available via the **Quality Index** widget. Navigate to **Dashboard** | **Quality Index** widget | **QI Complexity Bar**

The formula for the QI Complexity metric is:

(Complexity > 30 *10 + Complexity > 20 * 5 + Complexity > 10 * 3 + Complexity > 1) / effective lines of code

Design metrics

Abstractness and Instability design metrics as specified by Robert C. Martin have not been implemented yet; however, there is an open ticket by the Sonar development team at `http://jira.codehaus.org/browse/SONAR-94`.

Metric name	Definition	Sonar component
Abstractness	The ratio of the number of abstract classes (and interfaces) to the total number of classes in the analyzed package.	To be implemented – open ticket SONAR-94.
Afferent couplings	Number of other classes that use this class.	These are available via the Sonar Sourcecode viewer Drill down to **Class level	Open in Sourcecode viewer	Dependencies** tab.
Depth in tree (DIT)	Number of parent classes.	To be implemented – open ticket SONAR-94
Efferent couplings	Number of classes that are used by this class.	This is available via the Sonar source code viewer. Drill down to **Class level	Open in Sourcecode viewer	Dependencies** tab
File dependencies to cut	Total number of dependencies between files.	This is available via the **Package Design** widget. Navigate to **Dashboard	Package Design** widget	**Total dependencies between files**.
Instability	The number of classes inside a package that depend on classes outside the package.	This is available via the Sonar source code viewer. Drill down to **Class level	Open in Sourcecode viewer	Dependencies** tab

Metric name	Definition	Sonar component
Lack of cohesion of methods (LCOM4)	Correlation between the methods and the local instance variables of a class. Methods not related to local fields increase the class LCOM number by one.	These are available via the Sonar source code viewer. Drill down to **Class level | Open in Sourcecode viewer | LCOM4** tab Alternatively, navigate to **Dashboard | Chidamber and Kemerer** widget | **Files having LCOM4 greater than 1**.
Number of Children (NOC)	Number of descendants of the class.	This is available via the Sonar source code viewer Drill down to **Class level | Open in Sourcecode viewer | Source** tab (on the left-hand side of the header)
Package cycles	The minimum number of package cycles detected while traversing a package to identify dependencies.	These are available via the **Package Design** widget. Navigate to **Dashboard | Package Design** widget | **Total cycles**.
Package dependencies to cut	Total number of dependencies between packages.	This is available via the **Package Design** widget. Navigate to **Dashboard | Package Design** widget | **Total dependencies between packages**.
Package tangle index	Level of tangle of the packages; the best is 0 percent.	This is available via the **Package Design** widget. Navigate to **Dashboard | Package Design** widget | **Package tangle index in percentage**.
Response For Class (RFC)	Total number of methods that can be potentially executed by an object of this class counting distinct calls made by the methods in the class.	This is available via the **Chidamber and Kemerer** widget. Navigate to **Dashboard | Chidamber and Kemerer** widget | **Response for Class | value/class**.

Documentation metrics

Documentation-related metrics are available via the **Comments and Duplications** widget.

Metric name	Definition	Sonar component
Blank comments	Empty comment lines.	These are available via the **Treemap**. Navigate to **Dashboard** | **Components** | Treemap on the right | **Set size to Blank Comments metric.**
Comment lines	Number of Javadoc, multi-comment, and single-comment lines. Empty comment lines, header file comments, and commented-out lines of code are not included.	These are available via the **Comments and Duplications** widget. Navigate to **Dashboard** | **Comments and Duplications** widget | **total lines.**
Commented-out LOC	Commented out lines of code. The Javadoc blocks are excluded.	This is available via the **Comments and Duplications** widget. Navigate to **Dashboard** | **Comments and Duplications** widget | **total commented LOCs.**
Density of Comments (%)	*Number of comment lines / (lines of code + number of comments lines) * 100.*	This is available via the **Comments and Duplications** widget. Navigate to **Dashboard** | **Comments and Duplications** widget | **comments percentage value.**
Density of Public documented API (%)	*(Number of public API - Number of undocumented public API) / Number of public API * 100.*	This is available via the **Comments and Duplications** widget. Navigate to **Dashboard** | **Comments and Duplications** widget | **documented API percentage value.**

Metric name	Definition	Sonar component
Public undocumented API	Number of public API without Javadoc.	This is available via the **Comments and Duplications** widget. Navigate to **Dashboard | Comments and Duplications** widget | **undocumented API total value.**

Duplication metrics

Duplication metrics are available via the **Comments and Duplications** widget and the Useless Code Tracker is available as a plugin.

Metric name	Definition	Sonar component
Duplicated blocks	*Number of comment lines / (lines of code + number of comments lines) * 100.*	This is available via the **Comments and Duplications** widget. Navigate to **Dashboard | Comments and Duplications** widget | **number of blocks.**
Duplicated files	Number of files containing duplicated code.	This is available via the **Comments and Duplications** widget. Navigate to **Dashboard | Comments and Duplications** widget | **number of files.**
Duplicated lines	Number of physical lines touched by duplication.	This is available via the **Comments and Duplications** widget. Navigate to **Dashboard | Comments and Duplications** widget | **number of lines.**
Density of duplicated lines (%)	*Duplicated lines / Physical lines * 100.*	This is available via the **Comments and Duplications** widget. Navigate to **Dashboard | Comments and Duplications** widget | **percentage value.**
Useless code	Total number of lines that can potentially be reduced via refactoring.	This is available via the **Useless Code Tracker** widget. Navigate to **Dashboard | Useless Code Tracker** widget | **total number of useless LOCs.**

General metrics

The Quality Index metric is available through the Quality Index plugin. Install it from `http://docs.codehaus.org/display/SONAR/Quality+Index+Plugin` or from **Sonar Update Center | Plugin Library**.

Metric name	Definition	Sonar component
Profile version	Version of the Sonar analysis profile.	This is available via the **Description** widget. Navigate to **Dashboard	Description** widget	**Profile Version value**.
Quality Index	A value on scale of 0 to 10 based on the following four weighted axes of quality: Coding Violations, Complexity, Coverage, and Checkstyle Standards	This is available via the **Quality Index** widget. Navigate to **Dashboard	Quality Index Widget	Total Quality value**.

Code Coverage and Unit Test metrics

Code Coverage and Unit Test metrics are displayed with the **Coverage** widget from the project dashboard. In differential mode, the widget reports only on new/updated code, as you can see in the following screenshot:

Code coverage
30.2% (-0.7)
29.5% line coverage (-1.0)
32.3% branch coverage (-0.1)

On new code:
3.8%
370 lines to cover
3.0% line coverage
8.9% branch coverage

Unit test success
99.0% (-1.0)
8 failures (+8)
0 errors (+0)
767 tests (+158)
4 skipped (+0)
5:38 min (+1:19 min)

In the following table, the Sonar Component column is omitted because all metrics are available from the same widget—the **Code Coverage** widget.

Metric name	Definition
Branch Coverage	Percentage value of covered branches in program flow structures (Boolean expressions).
Coverage	Percentage value of total coverage combining line and branch coverage.
Line Coverage	Percentage value of number of lines executed/covered in unit tests.
Lines to cover	Total number of uncovered LOCs in unit tests.
New branch coverage	As Branch Coverage but only for new/updated code.
New branches to cover	Total number of uncovered branches only in new/updated code.
New coverage	As Coverage but only for new/updated code.
New line coverage	As Line Coverage but only for new/updated code.
New lines to cover	As Lines to cover but only for new/updated code.
Uncovered branches	Total number of branches not covered by unit tests.
Uncovered lines	Total number of lines of code that are not covered by unit tests.
New uncovered branches	As Uncovered branches to cover but only for new/updated code.
New uncovered lines	As Uncovered lines to cover but only for new/updated code.
Skipped unit tests	Number of skipped unit tests.
Unit tests	Total number of unit tests.
Unit test errors	Number of unit test errors—assertion errors.
Unit test failures	Number of unit tests that failed with an unhandled exception.
Unit test success (%)	Percentage value of successful unit tests—excluding errors and failures.
Unit tests duration	Total duration of unit tests' execution time.

The formula for the Coverage metric as implemented by the Sonar development team is:

Coverage = (CT + CF + LC) / (2*B + EL)

Where:

- *CT*: Branches that evaluated to `true` at least once
- *CF*: Branches that evaluated to `false` at least once
- *LC*: Lines covered (`lines_to_cover` - `uncovered_lines`)
- *B*: Total number of branches (2*B = `conditions_to_cover`)
- *EL*: Total number of executable lines (`lines_to_cover`)

Rules Compliance metrics

You can review Rules and Violations metrics from the project dashboard by using the default **Rules Compliance** widget and Useless Code Tracker with Quality Index widgets available as plugins. Notice that the widgets report on new violations and metric values when in differential mode for new/updated code.

Metric name	Definition	Sonar component
Rules Compliance	Weighted violations percentage value.	This is available via the **Rules Compliance** widget. Navigate to **Dashboard | Rules Compliance** widget | percentage value
Violations	Total number of code violations.	This is available via the **Rules Compliance** widget. Navigate to **Dashboard | Rules Compliance widget | Total number**
Weighted Violations	*Total sum of weighted violations (number of violations * weight value)*	This is available via the **Rules Compliance** widget. Navigate to **Dashboard | Rules Compliance** widget.
Blocker Violations	Total value of Blocker level code violations.	This is available via the **Rules Compliance** widget. **Navigate to Dashboard | Rules Compliance** widget | **Blocker.**

Metric name	Definition	Sonar component
Critical Violations	Total value of Critical-level code violations.	This is available via the **Rules Compliance** widget. Navigate to **Dashboard** | **Rules Compliance** widget | **Critical**
Major Violations	Total value of Major-level code violations.	This is available via the **Rules Compliance** widget. Navigate to **Dashboard** | **Rules Compliance** widget | **Major**.
Minor Violations	Total value of Minor-level code violations.	This is available via the **Rules Compliance** widget. Navigate to **Dashboard** | **Rules Compliance** widget | **Minor**.
Info Violations	Total value of Info-level code violations.	This is available via the **Rules Compliance** widget. Navigate to **Dashboard** | **Rules Compliance** widget | **Info**.
New Blocker Violations	Same as Blocker Violations but for new/updated code only.	This is available via the **Rules Compliance** widget. Navigate to **Dashboard** | **Rules Compliance** widget | **Blocker in differential mode**.
New Critical Violations	Same as Critical violations but for new/updated code only.	This is available via the **Rules Compliance** widget. Navigate to **Dashboard** | **Rules Compliance** widget | **Critical in differential mode**.
New Major Violations	Same as Info violations but for new/updated code only.	This is available via the **Rules Compliance** widget. Navigate to **Dashboard** | **Rules Compliance** widget | **Major in differential mode**.

Metric name	Definition	Sonar component
New Minor Violations	Same as Major violations but for new/updated code only.	This is available via the **Rules Compliance** widget. Navigate to **Dashboard | Rules Compliance** widget | **Minor in differential mode.**
New Info Violations	Same as Minor violations but for new/updated code only.	This is available via the **Rules Compliance** widget. Navigate to **Dashboard | Rules Compliance** widget | **Info in differential mode.**
New Violations	Total number of violations in new code only.	This is available via the **Rules Compliance** widget. Navigate to **Dashboard | Rules Compliance** widget | **Added in differential mode.**
Dead Code	Total lines of code in unused private methods.	This is available via the **Useless Code Tracker** widget. Navigate to **Dashboard | Useless Code Tracker** widget | **total number of LOCs.**
Potential Dead Code	Total lines of code in unused protected methods.	This is available via the **Useless Code Tracker** widget. Navigate to **Dashboard | Useless Code Tracker** widget | **total number of LOCs.**
Quality Index Coding Weighted Violations	Quality Index on Coding violations calculated is by the formula: *(Blocker * 10 + Critical * 5 + Major * 3 + Minor + Info) / LOCs*	This is available via the **Quality Index** widget. Navigate to **Dashboard | Quality Index** widget | **Coding Bar.**
Quality Index Style Weighted Violations	Quality Index on Checkstyle violations is calculated by the formula: *QI Style = (Errors*10 + Warnings) / LOCs * 10*	This is available via the **Quality Index** widget. Navigate to **Dashboard | Quality Index** widget | **Style Bar.**

Size metrics

The following metrics are displayed in the **Size** widget from the project dashboard. On the left-hand side of the widget there is information on line levels and statements, while on the right-hand side of the widget there is information on packages and classes.

Metric name	Definition
Accessors	Number of getter and setter methods.
Classes	Number of classes including nested classes, interfaces, enums, and annotations.
Directories	Number of analyzed directories.
Files	Number of analyzed files.
Lines	Number of carriage returns.
Lines of code	Number of physical lines of code excluding blanks, comments, and commented-out code.
Methods	Total number of methods excluding accessors.
Packages	Total number of packages.
Statements	Total number of statements.
	The statements counter gets incremented by one each time one of the following is encountered:
	`expression`, `if`, `else`, `while`, `do`, `for`, `switch`, `break`, `continue`, `return`, `throw`, `synchronized`, `catch`, and `finally`.

Management metrics

The next three metrics are business oriented and you can add them to the **Custom Measures** widget. You can also add it to the dashboard.

Metric name	Definition
Burned Budget	The budget already used in the project.
Business Value	An indication of the value of the project to the business.
Team size	The size of the project team.

Index

F

G

H

I

J

Thank you for buying
Sonar Code Quality Testing Essentials

About Packt Publishing

Packt, pronounced 'packed', published its first book "*Mastering phpMyAdmin for Effective MySQL Management*" in April 2004 and subsequently continued to specialize in publishing highly focused books on specific technologies and solutions.

Our books and publications share the experiences of your fellow IT professionals in adapting and customizing today's systems, applications, and frameworks. Our solution based books give you the knowledge and power to customize the software and technologies you're using to get the job done. Packt books are more specific and less general than the IT books you have seen in the past. Our unique business model allows us to bring you more focused information, giving you more of what you need to know, and less of what you don't.

Packt is a modern, yet unique publishing company, which focuses on producing quality, cutting-edge books for communities of developers, administrators, and newbies alike. For more information, please visit our website: www.packtpub.com.

About Packt Open Source

In 2010, Packt launched two new brands, Packt Open Source and Packt Enterprise, in order to continue its focus on specialization. This book is part of the Packt Open Source brand, home to books published on software built around Open Source licences, and offering information to anybody from advanced developers to budding web designers. The Open Source brand also runs Packt's Open Source Royalty Scheme, by which Packt gives a royalty to each Open Source project about whose software a book is sold.

Writing for Packt

We welcome all inquiries from people who are interested in authoring. Book proposals should be sent to author@packtpub.com. If your book idea is still at an early stage and you would like to discuss it first before writing a formal book proposal, contact us; one of our commissioning editors will get in touch with you.

We're not just looking for published authors; if you have strong technical skills but no writing experience, our experienced editors can help you develop a writing career, or simply get some additional reward for your expertise.

Learn by doing: less theory, more results

Selenium 1.0
Testing Tools

Test your web applications with multiple browsers using the
Selenium Framework to ensure the quality of web applications

Beginner's Guide

David Burns [ ] open source

Selenium 1.0 Testing Tools: Beginner's Guide

ISBN: 978-1-849510-26-4   Paperback: 232 pages

Test your web applications with multiple browsers
using the Selenium Framework to ensure the quality
of web applications

1. Save your valuable time by using Selenium to
   record, tweak and replay your test scripts

2. Get rid of any bugs deteriorating the quality of
   your web applications

3. Take your web applications one step closer to
   perfection using Selenium tests

4. Packed with detailed working examples that
   illustrate the techniques and tools for debugging

Quick answers to common problems

Jenkins Continuous
Integration Cookbook

Over 80 recipes to maintain, secure, communicate, test, build,
and improve the software development process with Jenkins

Alan Mark Berg [ ] open source

Jenkins Continuous Integration Cookbook

ISBN: 978-1-849517-40-9   Paperback: 344 pages

Over 80 recipes to maintain, secure, communicate,
test, build, and improve the software development
process with Jenkins

1. Explore the use of more than 40 best of
   breed plugins

2. Use code quality metrics, integration testing
   through functional and performance testing to
   measure the quality of your software

3. Get a problem-solution approach enriched
   with code examples for practical and easy
   comprehension

Please check **www.PacktPub.com** for information on our titles

Apache Maven 3 Cookbook

ISBN: 978-1-849512-44-2   Paperback: 224 pages

Over 50 recipes towards optimal Java software engineering with Maven 3

1. Grasp the fundamentals and extend Apache Maven 3 to meet your needs

2. Implement engineering practices in your application development process with Apache Maven

3. Collaboration techniques for Agile teams with Apache Maven

4. Use Apache Maven with Java, Enterprise Frameworks, and various other cutting-edge technologies

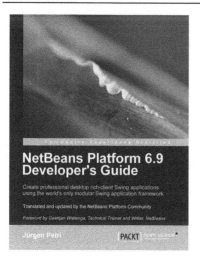

NetBeans Platform 6.9 Developer's Guide

ISBN: 978-1-849511-76-6   Paperback: 288 pages

Create professional desktop rich-client Swing applications using the world's only modular Swing application framework

1. Create large, scalable, modular Swing applications from scratch

2. Master a broad range of topics essential to have in your desktop application development toolkit, right from conceptualization to distribution

3. Pursue an easy-to-follow sequential and tutorial approach that builds to a complete Swing application

Please check **www.PacktPub.com** for information on our titles